Y0-CPF-608

A WALK THROUGH MY GARDEN

EDITED & DESIGNED
BY
WHITNEY SCOTT

OUTRIDER PRESS, INC.
DYER, INDIANA

ALL CHARACTERS, SITUATIONS AND SETTINGS IN
THIS COLLECTION'S FICTION ARE IMAGINARY

A WALK THROUGH MY GARDEN IS PUBLISHED BY
OUTRIDER PRESS IN AFFILIATION WITH
TALLGRASS WRITERS GUILD.

TRADEMARKS AND BRAND NAMES HAVE BEEN PRINTED IN
INITIAL CAPITAL LETTERS

BOOK DESIGN & PRODUCTION
BY
WHITNEY SCOTT

© 2007, OUTRIDER PRESS, INC
ISBN 0-9712903-3-4

OUTRIDER PRESS, INC
2036 NORTH WINDS DRIVE
DYER, INDIANA 46311

ALL RIGHTS RESERVED
PRINTED IN THE UNITED STATES
10 9 8 7 6 5 4 3 2 1

ONCE AGAIN, TO LEE CUNNINGHAM, FOR HER EXCEPTIONAL DEDICATION TO THIS
SERIES WITH HER OUTSTANDING BEHIND-THE-SCENES SUPPORT.

CONTENTS

✿▩▨✿

PROSE WINNERS

GRAND PRIZE
THE FALL BY UTE CARSON

2ND PLACE
THE MAN WHO GREW IN MY
GARDEN BY LAURIE DOLLOCK

3RD PLACE
TIME CAPSULE BY HARKER
BRAUTIGHAN

HONORABLE MENTION
LATE WINTER JOURNEY INTO
SPRINGTIM BY CARLA A. FELLERS

HONORABLE MENTION
HOMECOMING BY AMBER KENMPPAINEN

HONORABLE MENTION
IN THE GARDEN BY DEANNA HOPPER

POETRY WINNERS

GRAND PRIZE
SEPTEMBER NUMBERS BY MARY DINGEE
FILLMORE

2ND PLACE
TAKING THAT BITE ... BY SUSAN
BALLER-SHEPARD

3RD PLACE
BOX OF DISQUIET BY CAROL CARPENTER

HONORABLE MENTION
FROM A SLIGHTLY MASOCHISTIC
PETUNIA BY MARY BAST

HONORABLE MENTION
HOUSEPLANT BY LYNN FITZGERALD

HONORABLE MENTION
MEMORIAL GARDEN BY PAM CROW

10

A BLOOM OF RAVE REVIEWS

BRET ANGELOS

[Recorded at the 2006 International Congress on Mad Science in Toronto, Ontario]

MY TIME WILL come. For me, this is a foregone conclusion and it will happen sooner rather than later. No need to boo, ladies and gentlemen. A little pomposity and bombast is to be expected in our collective field. I'm simply stating that "My time will come" is a belief that has been held by many of the world's unrecognized greats. Talent is often trapped below the waves in air pockets that can take ages to finally surface. Once these talent bubbles emerge, pure happenstance often determines if anyone is there to note the results. It is the same for every discipline, be it art, philosophy, science, or engineering. Even my own distant ancestor, Gregor Mendel, was heard to remark shortly before his death, "My time will come."

 This slideshow and presentation will present to you the sum total of my life's work. As I mentioned earlier, I am a distant relative of Gregor Mendel, whose work has had a great impact on my own. Who was this Gregor Mendel? Born in Austria in the 1800's, he took up residence at the Abbey of St. Thomas where he began a journey of discovery involving the simple garden pea. Some call Gregor Mendel the founder of modern genetics. Others call him a diligent and meticulous recorder of details, a science writer, if you will. I call him the world's greatest gardener. Over the course of a decade, he tended and cared for over 28,000 pea plants. He peered at each one with the inquisitive eye of a scientist noting the changes in each generation and carefully crossbreeding different strains to witness the effects. It took many years but his time did come. Gregor Mendel, the world's greatest gardener/scrivener, had given us insight into the basic functions of heredity.

 I remember fondly when my father gave me my first Gregor Mendel Pea Plant Kit. It sold terribly in the stores, but that was only because of the ignorance of the general populous. Like Gregor Mendel, I planted my green pea plants and my yellow pea plants, tended to them lovingly and watched the traits of each new generation change. As a child I began to wonder what other special genes these wondrous plants could possess. Over time I became interested in much more than the simple garden pea. If this simple garden pea could teach us about human heredity, then I posited that there might be a plant that reveals deeper human secrets. There could be a plant or a flower that would reveal the most precious secret of all:how we humans ended up developing a written language while the rest of the animal kingdom was left to peeps, grunts, and sonic echoes. I'm talking about a plant that once caused man to pick up the stylus and etch out those first symbols in the clay. What I'm saying is that ancient writings might be somehow connected to the plants and flowers of their times.

You are thinking that this idea is pure madness. It would be impossible for a mere plant to affect the genes of a human being in such a way. So much has been said of the scientifically impossible over the years. While I respect and secretly disdain many of my esteemed colleagues here today, I prefer to see the impossible as yet another opportunity for Mad Science.

For years I scoured the globe searching for these special and exotic plants. My search naturally focused on the Middle East as it was the cradle of civilization. I spent years examining reeds along the Nile River. I floated on the saltwater of the Dead Sea looking for lilies. A milkweed on the Persian Gulf seemed promising, but ultimately proved disappointing. My efforts were hampered as much of this area is a war zone. Attempts to travel in modern day Iraq were obviously dangerous and difficult. I was beginning to lose hope, but that's when my luck changed.

A U.S. Air Force bombing run had revealed ancient ruins deep within one of the blast craters. Miraculously, these ruins remained buried and perfectly intact. I like to refer to this stroke of good fortune as the world's first example of aerial bombardment archaeology. Clay tablets covered in cuneiform writing were recovered along with a plethora of common household items. This village was obviously established by ancient Sumerians, one of the earliest civilizations to possess a written language. Of interest to me were some preserved seeds recovered from a clay jar. After some discreet haggling with the Iraqi government involving a large cash layout and some low-grade weapons research, I was able to obtain all of these precious seeds.

The seeds were still viable and I quickly planted my first batch. After ten days I began to notice the first hints of green poking above the surface. As you can see from this next slide, this ancient plant resembles a spider flower. I determined that this plant was a distant relative of Cleome Hasslerana. Cleome gets its nickname "Spider Flower" from the spider-like flowers with long, waving stamen which are held on tall, strong leafy stems. It's an annual that makes its home comfortably among shrubs and perennials. When planted in mass, they look like blooming shrubbery with eight-inch balls of blossoms and can reach a height of six feet in a good season. They also tolerate heat and dry weather well, which makes them perfectly suited for the Middle Eastern climate.

I kept these ancient flowers in my private garden laboratory. This greenhouse is completely sealed off from the outside world. I needed to keep my spider flowers pure and unspoiled by the vagaries of our own time. When tending to my new flowers, I wore a clean suit that would prevent any contamination from my own person. This first sample batch of flowers were grown and blossomed in exactly the same way that they did almost five thousand years ago. I raised several generations of the flowers and then examined their internal structures to make sure that they were maintaining their genetic integrity. Each generation was identical to the first batch and I knew that I had raised a pure strain of this ancient plant.

It was now up to me to determine if this plant had any peculiar effects on animal life. I compared its structure to modern Cleome Hasslerana and determined that a certain portion of the genetic code of this old plant had been lost in the modern equivalent. Evolution might have proclaimed this code obsolete and deleted it, but I suspected that this was, in fact, the code that made this plant special. My first tests were conducted using chimpanzees.

The chimps, our evolutionary cousins, might be affected in a similar manner by the spider flowers. I noticed that as each chimp entered the test area, they immediately approached the bright purple blossoms and breathed deeply. The aroma of these plants was obviously quite stimulating. It was so stimulating, in fact, that several of the chimps proceeded to destroy my precious flowers in due course. After each destructive episode, each chimp would smile at me and flash its pearly whites. I was not amused but I continued my research. Time and effort produced results for my great ancestor, Gregor Mendel, and the same work ethic would aid my quest. I continued thinking to myself, "My time will come."

I had used six different chimps during the experiment. I placed toys, books, puzzles, paper, and other objects of amusement in the test area with the chimpanzees. Gradually there was less and less destruction of the plants by the chimps and more focus on the other items in the test area. Of special note was a young chimp named Symbaal. I was shocked to discover that he had correctly solved a Rubik's Cube one afternoon. Thinking that this was mere chance, I introduced another Rubik's Cube and Symbaal solved it in half an hour. This was a feat that I, Doctor Ivan Mendel, Professor of Paleo-Botany at Reykjavic University and Genetics Fellow at the Zurich College of Medicine, had never achieved despite numerous attempts. I kept a watchful eye on Symbaal as he studied the books arrayed around the spider flower. Symbaal already had a rudimentary understanding of sign language and he kept signing the symbol for "teach me." Stunned, I entered the room in my clean suit and commenced Symbaal's lessons in the Queen's English.

You will no doubt dismiss Symbaal's accomplishments as mere chance. Permit me to introduce you to him this instant. As you can see, he has a tiny keyboard attached to his forearm. This keyboard allows Symbaal to communicate using a voice synthesizer. I say, Symbaal: how are you doing today?

"Quite well, Doctor. How are you?"

Please, people! Please! Remain calm. I never would have suspected such cries of witchcraft and devilry from the likes of this International Congress on Mad Science. I know for a fact that several of you present today in this audience have done things much worse. My only crime is giving a chimpanzee with a talent for typing the opportunity to understand what he was banging out on the keyboard. My young Symbaal is a far better writer than the lot of you and in time, you will come to respect his prowess on the keys.

14

Symbaal informed me that it was the spider flower that caused this breakthrough in his consciousness. I was intrigued and finally decided to throw caution to the wind and expose myself to these ancient plants. I asked Symbaal to call the hospital should the blossoms prove poisonous to human beings. When I entered the test area, I was immediately struck by the pungent aroma emanating from the spider flowers. I was drawn to them. Like a feline rolling in catnip, I felt compelled to rub the plants all over my own person. Slide 232-b shows a nice image of me flashing my own pearly whites as if in a drug-induced euphoria. After several weeks, I also stopped destroying the plants and began to notice a distinctive change in my own human consciousness.

All distractions were eliminated from my life. There was no radio. There was no television. There was no Internet. My existence was reduced to a pad and a pencil. I began to write. For months I scratched out page after page. I lost 20 pounds for lack of eating. My only nourishment came from pondering life's many questions and writing down my own answers.

There was no field left untouched by my imaginings. These ancient spider flowers had provided me with my own personal Renaissance and I had provided them with a new name. They would be known for time immemorial as Corrolarium Humanitas or Culture Blossoms.

The search was on for plants containing a similar line of genetic code as the Culture Blossoms. For the last ten years, Symbaal and I have traveled the globe looking for this lost sequence. It was an arduous and exhaustive search. We canoed down the Amazon. We backpacked in the Himalayas. We tried a little walkabout in the Great Sandy desert in Australia. Symbaal learned French and German, and I acquired a certain proficiency in both Mandarin and Cantonese. After all of these travels, I am proud to say that we were very successful.

We not only found plants similar to the ancient spider flowers, we also bred them with each other. We have created numerous highly specialized hybrids. Each plant is completely harmless to both human and chimpanzee alike, but offers a variety of very specific enhancements to the test subject. Symbaal and I have determined that the aroma of these plants combined with the almost imperceptible oils coating the blossoms act in such a way as to "turn on" certain genes common to both human and chimp. Curiously, the expression of these genes provide enhancements that are literary in nature.

15

So, it is with great pleasure that I introduce to the members of this great International Congress all of the Mendel-Symbaal lines of Corrolarium Humanitas. You may obtain a license to these lines for an appropriate fee.

Slide 303-A contains a flower which causes the test subject to immediately produce a high quality memoir suitable for publication. My own memoir, *My Only Friend Is A Chimp*, is available in the lobby for just $23.99. My associate, Symbaal, is still shopping his memoir around for an appropiate publisher.

This next flower creates an unstoppable urge to write handwritten correspondence to distant relatives and acquaintances. The creation of homemade greeting cards is also a curious by-product. A related companion flower causes the subject to write exquisitely crafted "Dear John" or "Dear Jane" letters that are always carefully calculated to let the other person down easy.

Mendel-Symbaal Flower-242 causes the subject to produce sequels better than the original. Symbaal is currently working on a brilliant new work. How's it going, Symbaal?

"It's going swimmingly. My new play, *Hamlet II: The Real Revenge*, should be on Broadway next Christmas."

Excellent! An infinite number of typing monkeys might be able to write Shakespeare over the course of an eternity but a right-thinking chimp can do it within a year. Chimps really know how to stay on deadline.

There are dozens more varieties available offering many of the popular genres, such as mysteries, romance, action-thrillers, legal-thrillers, techno-legal thrillers, satires, comedies, sci-fi, westerns, historical epics, biographies, poems, odes, haiku, limericks, and other bawdy tales. With this new series of Culture Blossoms, a writer does not have to lament to him or herself, "My time will come." Simple exposure to the flowers will produce unparalleled results that will guarantee success.

So, ladies and gentlemen of the International Congress on Mad Science, permit me to show you first-hand the newest Culture Blossom available from Mendel-Symbaal Incorporated. It is known in common parlance as "A Bloom of Rave Reviews," and I'm sure that the news media present today will take a fine liking to them. My associate, Symbaal, will present each of you with a complimentary sample.

Symbaal, if you will.

16

FROM A SLIGHTLY MASOCHISTIC PETUNIA

MARY BAST

I'm so sexy I could spit!
Please notice my dark, velvety tongue
   lapping at the ground, lightly.
Ah! Deep-throated cry:
   My want poisons me.

Stay with me, snap my blossom,
   please, while I am coming
   down from passion,
   or I'll die, lie dormant.
The idea of a swaying, living bloom.

17

GARDEN IN AUTUMN

MARY BLINN

They lose their strength these last few weeks
shriveled, spotted, translucent in the incidental
light of brown October, resigned to display a
different, bony kind of beauty; listen to a
wisdom hidden deep in the root that whispers
your work is complete
your season has passed.
So I, too, must respond to the hardened ground
the dry rattle of autumn and reluctant, tend to
their winter bed, ready them for the cold sleep
ahead and for me, long months of remembering
the stain of green on my fingers
the smell of earth in my hands.

TIME CAPSULE

HARKER BRAUTIGHAN

I IMAGINE THEM replanting the garden sometimes. It's a couple, usually, a man and a woman. I make them a straight couple, I suppose, because the woman might understand. But in the old days, before they moved, I worried about Drew and Martin putting in some new plants. Martin would get this look on his face that would say, without words, "I don't want to know."

Drew would take over, saying, "Oh my God. What on Earth is this? What the hell? I mean, really, what the hell?" Then he'd call me up and whisper, conspiratorially, into the phone, "Girl, you've got to come down here and see what someone's buried in the garden."

A group of my friends and family sat in a circle on my bedroom floor, the room that I had once shared with him. The room was so small and so crowded, more crowded now that I was alone than it had ever been with him there. The ocean that separates us was always there in that room, the bed empty even when he was crushed against me, my vulva reaching back, hungry, greedy, lonely, kissing his cock all night long. I no longer dream of sex. Last night, I dreamed I was in a shop. I wanted to try on clothes, but I didn't know where to set my vibrator down while I went into the fitting room. Is that the way sex ends? That even dreams and fantasies lack imagination for anything but masturbation?

The bed was always empty when Robert and I together lay side by side in it, our hands clasped next to our clutching bodies. The bed held nothing but people in the end, and people alone can't fill up a bed. Beds need to be ploughed and furrowed, and beds need dreams. Dormant dreams yield withered fruit as Mr. Hughes taught us so long ago.

Now my dreams are haunted by the dead, who so lovingly frequent those empty middle hours. The dead have taken the place of my dead love, my dead past. They take up Robert's side of the bed, lying beside me, as solid as his cock against my back.

On my thirtieth birthday, Robert gave me diamond earrings and seemed astonished, perhaps embarrassed, when I thought the gift meant our relationship was getting more serious. We both underestimated the brainwashing power of DeBeers.

A diamond is forever.

When I was a teenager, I was abused by an older man, Frank. He gave me a heart-shaped pendant with little diamonds all over it. Years later, I was moving out of my home, and I found that awful little heart, along with some earrings and a rhinestone necklace I'd loved for years. Suddenly, it occurred to me that however much I liked the necklace and tiger's eye earrings, and as reluctant as I was to throw away diamonds, there was something existentially malignant about keeping the gifts of a man who'd left me with scars more durable than diamonds.

In the middle hours, the hours of the dead, I walked the labyrinth in my yard with a Wicca high priestess. Taking a bundle of feathers and some sage from her bag, she lit the sage and smudged me with the smoke. The breezy feathers and smoke contrasted with the weight of Brigid's deep, melodic voice. Putting the sage down, she invoked the four cardinal directions, and above and below, to form a circle around us and to bless our activity. She invited Kali, Durga and Kwan-Yin to lend me their ferocity, strength and compassion. She held my head in her hands, chanting and praying. I liked the solid presence of her hands on my face. Taking the candle that shape-shifted in the corner, Brigid led me outside, over the threshold and onto my labyrinth. The night was cool. The smell of the redwoods hung damp in the hollow night. Under the guidance of Brigid's incantations, the night filled up. The shape of the symbol for woman, for life—an ankh—my labyrinth spiraled to the center of a womb. The redwoods midwifed my rebirth in the woods. In the center of the circle, Brigid placed a bowl before me on the ground. "I declare that the spirit of Frank, symbolized by this jewelry, is banished from the life, mind, and soul of this woman. His hold on her is cheap and weak, like the links in this tawdry chain." I broke the rhinestone necklace, once, twice, then crumbled it. "I declare that the words and deeds that have poisoned her heart are removed and expelled, like the diamonds we pluck from this pendant." As I pried the diamond shards out of the face of the smooth, silver heart, I noticed the pits I'd opened up.

When the jewelry was broken, I placed it in the bowl. Squatting over it, I cleansed myself by pissing what was good and hot and clean from my own body onto the traces of a man who had pissed all over my past.

With scraps of metal, glass, and stone, warm and redolent of earth, Brigid and I set off for the ocean, to cast the cleansed jewelry and

20

defiled memories out to sea. We were greeted by locked gates, a lone buck standing sentry. By the time we traced our way back to the road, then to mouth of the river, it was midnight. The hour of new beginnings. The death of night and the birth of day. I stood on the jetty jutting out into the bay, watching the river rush into the sea. A perfect threshold. A dozen bats held me in their sway, dancing with the night. They swooped and soared and sounded, their ethereal song brushing my shoulders. Together, we choreographed redemption as I jettisoned Frank's jewels along the arc of their flight.

On my thirty-first birthday, my loved ones gathered in my bedroom, around a big flower pot. We were planting a new life for me. Katya had written, "You are a rainbow of light," on the inside of the pot, and Dave placed a picture of me, laughing with my arms flung wide, beneath those words. The flower pot went around the room, receiving a seed from each person in the circle. Susan planted worry dolls, to take over worrying for me at night, so I could get some sleep. My brother laid a penny in the bottom, to help me grow prosperous. Dan, whose life fit him so loosely, dropped in the cornerstone that would sprout into a house of my own. Katya planted a new story. Linda gave me back my song.

Earlier that night, we had buried the remnants of my old life in the garden. I'd read about a native tradition, when a potter dies, of breaking his pottery to release his soul from it. Robert wasn't dead, and he hadn't made the pottery he gave me—he'd picked it up at a garage sale—but, close enough. Any ritual that involved a hammer couldn't be all bad. There was the requisite photograph. And the last article of clothing, still pushed in the corner under "his" side of the bed.

I can still almost hear Drew on the phone. "Get down here. Right now. Some lunatic's planted a voodoo box in the garden...no, really, you've got to see this...there's a picture—and honey, I think you're in it—and some broken dishes...and this is the part that really takes the cake—the whole thing's wrapped up in a pair of men's underwear! You should see Martin's face right now. He's just shaking his head. What, Martin? Unbelievable? Yeah, I know, that's what I'm telling her. I think it's funny. Oh, come off it, Martin, you know it's funny. Hey, are you still there? I bet it was those awful tenants on the second floor—the ones who got evicted. How scary. Girl, they've got a picture here, and I swear that's your hair...I can't tell; it's only half a picture and I can't see the man's face anymore. I can't tell whether to laugh or freak out. Either way, you better get down here, girl, before I pee my pants."

HARVEST

MICHELLE Y. BURKE

Love, do not draw back now.
I want to slip the golden flesh of summer into your body,
squash buttered and cubed. *Delicata, Buttercup.*
I need to nourish you.
Another may offer a rose,
a perfect pear, a prayer to taste on your tongue at night.
All bruise. We each turn to god and find
emptiness. Rosary beads blacken. Lips grow pale,
and twined embraces, robust in summer heat,
succumb to cold. Still I call you
Beloved. The sun, mutable star, hardens husks,
turning insides gold.

THE BLOODY PULP

BONNIE JO CAMPBELL

LOOSE TOMATOES ROLL off countertops and splat on the tiled floor. I pick them up and cut away the ruined spots with my wooden-handled paring knife, the one that feels just right in my hand, the one Christopher sharpens for me on a stone. The seedy contents of sealed jars beside the sink have separated into transparent juice like plasma and red flesh. Dishtowels are strewn about with blood-colored stains on them. There is nowhere to put a bag of groceries or a hot pan after removing it from the stove. I flag down my neighbor Lynne on the dirt road and tell her, "Come, take tomatoes. Take all you can use so I can find room to slice an onion." I carry tomatoes wherever I go, quart-sized yogurt containers full of the small ones: red cherry, orange cherry, grape, yellow pear-shaped.

23

Shortly after our August wedding 18 years ago, my mother gave Christopher a framed *New Yorker* cartoon by Gahan Wilson. The caption reads: "Here comes your tomato surprise, sir." As the waiter stands poised to lift the lid, a dozen tomatoes wielding axes are climbing the man's chair. This is how my husband feels at this time of year, when tomatoes cover every surface, clog every drain, when every sweep of his gaze takes in a seed-smeared patina of tomato pulp. Christopher does not like tomatoes; his mother told me that from toddlerhood, he threw back at her any food containing even miniscule amounts of the tomato. Nowadays he pushes his glasses up onto his forehead and reads the ingredients list on the side of every cracker package that enters our home, to make sure that powder of tomato is not lurking down near the bottom of the list. Nonetheless, at this time of year, he inhales the stuff night and day.

I do not have bathroom guest towels—you can dry your hands on one of Christopher's dirty T-shirts the same as I do—but I do have guest tomatoes. If you visit, I will present you with flawless fruits, the loveliest ones, optimal in ripeness, Brandywines even, or Romas if you want to make a sauce. For myself I prefer to eat the damaged fruits; I get joy out of salvaging the ones with bug holes, the ones that are so swollen with juice that they crack. The birds and woodchucks eat some of my tomatoes, but I don't really care. I have 42 plants.

Praise goodness, so far there are no tomato hornworms in my garden. I've seen them in other women's gardens, and the word worms hardly does them justice. At four inches long and horned, we might call them tomato snakes, tomato dragons, tomato demons. I do not use chemicals in my garden, so in order to keep the insects away, I can only strive to be a good person and keep my heart as pure as practically possible. My sister-in-law's tomato worms were undoubtedly brought on by her failure to love my brother properly. As I see it, from the time the worms appeared on her plants, it was a steady decline to her leaving him and moving back into her parents' basement. As I admire my garden, I vow to never belittle my husband or to demand he satisfy the messier of my emotional needs.

My tomatoes grow in a substrate of black swamp muck, trucked-in sand, and donkey manure, through holes I have punched in three-foot wide strips of black plastic. Between those rows I have piled hay and more donkey manure, eliminating most of the need for weeding and keeping me organic. So far nobody from the prison has complained about the manure smell.

See, my garden is actually closer to the minimum-security women's prison than to my own house. To get to my garden I follow a path a few hundred yards through the woods. As well as tomatoes, I grow peppers, eggplant, summer squash, winter squash, a few cucumbers, onions, turnip greens; French sorrel and parsley and burnett for salads; herbs like tarragon, oregano, sage, thyme, savory; lavender; St. John's wort (in case I get depressed); pennyroyal (for girls in trouble), stevia (for sweetening tea); and all kinds of mint (spearmint, peppermint, lemon balm, catnip), but that's all small potatoes (I do not grow potatoes; that is not my style).

Sometimes the prisoners come out for a smoke break while I'm picking tomatoes or weeding. They're not supposed to shout or wave to me, though a few can't resist. Seeing them makes me appreciate my freedom, especially my freedom to grow tomatoes, as many as I want, even way too many. I sometimes press the buzzer on the door that allows me entry into a locked vestibule and leave boxes of tomatoes for the gals, so that they will remember freedom. The only freedom they express now is the freedom to smoke. On Sunday they get an extended afternoon smoke break, during which some lounge on the lawn, others hug their knees on the curb, some chat while others remain silent. All of them smoke. So far, the prison officials have allowed my tomatoes ingress. My tomatoes have made their way to the inside, even those too juicy and ripe to be conducive to orderly conduct.

One day recently I was approaching my garden on the woods path, and a dark-haired girl was stepping over piles of lawn clippings and tree trimmings, determinedly headed toward the woods, not even seeing me because her dark bangs were in her eyes. Her arms were stiff from incarceration, but they were starting to loosen.

"Going somewhere?" I said. Her head jerked up so her bangs splashed against her forehead. Immediately I regretted speaking so authoritatively. Maybe I should have just hidden behind a tree and watched her go. Would she have run? If she'd followed the path, she would have ended up at my house. My wallet and car keys were on the dining room table and the door was unlocked. Somewhere in there we had a rifle and a shotgun. Or she might have stepped on a board with nails in it and sued us.

"This your woods?" she asked. I nodded yes. She said, "It makes me think of Wicca."

I turned around and looked at the woods, the view from the prison, different from my view from home, or the view from inside the woods. The lawn surrounding my garden gave way abruptly to swamp oaks and box elders with gnarled, mossy branches. Black raspberry brambles formed a living fence below. The woods were a wild place, thick with birdsong and seedpods. Poison ivy slithers up trees, and roots reached out to trip you if you weren't expecting them. Perhaps this girl was aware that tomatoes belong to the deadly nightshade family.

25

"Are you a witch?" I asked.

"I guess I should go back," she said, before I could offer her a tomato. She returned to the prison at a jog.

The minimum-security prison is brick, with a little stream running across the front, and when we first moved here it was a nursing home. Contrary to the guilty arrogance of the children and grandchildren who did not visit their elders there, the old and infirm in that place did not dream of their offspring. Most did not even dream of youth. When I became attuned to them, I discovered they dreamed of tomatoes. This was before I gardened, before I considered canning (though my mother canned and her mother and her mother's mother). Those neglected old folks dreamed tomato vines that snaked out through cracked windows, stretched through the woods, rattled my own windows and doors. Their tomato dreams awakened me early in the morning, even though Christopher works the late shift and I don't get to bed until after one o'clock. Those old folks dreamed so hard that I had to start breaking up the mucky clay outside their windows, hauling in sand and manure.

Those poor old folks lost their minds in those beds in those rooms where no fruit swelled or ripened in summer. They grasped in vain for favorite old wooden-handled paring knives, the ones they had sharpened on sharpening stones or had watched their husbands sharpen. Finally, in their endless and dull waking hours, they forgot the feel of good knives in their hands, forgot the taste of tomatoes warmed by the sun. One after another those old people died.

The prison girls have lost their freedom to grow tomatoes, have lost their access to sharp knives. Probably those girls weren't growing tomatoes even when they had the chance, and that is why they turned to drugs and smoking and breaking and entering and attempting to kill the men who treated them badly. Summer can be rife with trouble if a girl is not occupied by the right kind of flesh.

Box of Disquiet

Carol Carpenter

If you were here
you would see the bruises,
purple blossoms on my knees.

For you, I knelt all morning,
tugged weeds from April soil
so they would not seed again.

Nightshade roots dried white
in heat like your lies
wilted in the warm room where we slept.

I still remember the season of snow
when you left, how your tail lights blazed
red as two tulips against white.

Yellow daffodils opened at noon today
while I sipped chamomile tea, hoping
yellow petals would bring you back.

Even though I rid our garden of winter debris,
my heart is a box of disquiet,
buzzing with honey bees. Like you they sting.

28

THE FALL

UTE CARSON

THE MAY FRAGRANCE of apple blossoms wafted through the open window. I had propped my elbows on the windowsill of my upstairs bedroom and was gazing at myriads of pinkish petals illuminating the night like candles. Then I inhaled deeply with my eyes closed.

Mr. Franz's six sturdy apple trees bordered my mother's bountiful flower garden. A white picket fence divided our two properties, and a rusty iron gate hung loosely on its hinges. Low branches tapped it on windy days with an eerie persistence. The trees, all slightly different heights, stretched toward a changing sky. From my perch I could spy out over their tops. Without an official name for the golden sun-baked apples, we called them Paradise Apples.

29

The apple trees were planted in a semicircle and nothing was used as fertilizer but horse manure. The apples were the best I've ever eaten, firm and juicy. Although wide grease bands encircled the tree trunks to deter insects, the apple skins were pockmarked where worms had burrowed tunnels through them. But we didn't mind. My mother and father and my sister Inge and I grew healthy and strong on more than one apple a day.

Apples were part of our daily diet then, in Germany. At breakfast my mother sliced them onto our oatmeal. I took an apple to school in my backpack. Setting off to afternoon sports I ran under the low tree branches, grabbed an apple and sank my teeth into it without slowing down. Apples were often a staple at dinner. One dish of boiled apples and potatoes was called "Himmel und Erde" (heaven and earth). My mother prepared it with a roast seasoned with curry and thyme. My favorite apple dish was a dessert of baked apples filled with honey and almonds and sprinkled with cinnamon.

We made use of apples in many ways. We grated them for upset stomachs, pureed them into applesauce, and canned them. We ate whole apples, core and all. My parents explained to us that "the nutrients are

just under the protective envelope—the apple's skin—and in its heart."
The only time we pared apples was for a Sunday torte. I remember sitting across from my mother at the kitchen table and watching her fingers, quick as weasels, peel the skin off an apple in one long unbroken ringlet. She worked by feel without ever looking. Afterwards my sister and I gathered the peelings in a bucket and took them to the pond where from among the slimy algae ducks splashed toward the water's edge and gobbled up the apple curls which we dangled over their eager beaks.

Mr. and Mrs. Franz were generous neighbors and at harvest time we were all invited over to pick. My father helped Mr. Franz carry a heavy wooden ladder from tree trunk to tree trunk, its bottom raking the ground with a rustle of leaves. Then Father placed one foot on the lowest rung to steady the ladder as we took turns climbing up and filling our baskets which we set on the rung next to our feet. We hooked our bare toes around the slats. Sweat glistened under our armpits and along hairlines. Our waxy-brown calf muscles hardened as we balanced on tiptoe and reached. Once in a while an apple escaped our grasp and tumbled to the ground. Everyone laughed, "That's how Newton discovered gravity!"

I rested after filling several baskets and sat munching on a particularly crisp apple. Inge, who was finicky about eating, scolded me. "Don't crunch."

The apple trees were part of my life. We took our time growing.

We had picnics under those trees with blankets spread on the grass for extra softness. We laughed and talked under the thick dome of their leaves, and my little cousin Ralf used one of the lower branches to steady himself as he learned to walk.

May induced daydreaming to the accompaniment of buzzing bees busily gathering pollen. I remember being entangled by spider webs suspended between branches, feeling their fine transparent threads against my face.

One warm July evening Mr. Franz had his two little grandsons, Eric and Wolfgang, over. They giggled with the delight of small children, rolling apples back and forth on the lawn between their outspread legs.

With the arrival of October, light came through the branches at a slant and a rough wind ripped loose the blood-red leaves, then scattered them aflutter like a thousand flames. The bees returned, now drawn by the smell of overripe, decomposing fruit. The odor of damp air seeped into my clothes as I shook the branches, and the last apple stragglers which nestled among large serrated leaves fell to the ground.

With the first touch of frost and a nip in the air, my mother and Mrs. Franz circled through the trees in search of the strays and gathered them into their deep red, blue or checkered aprons which they held up by the corners. Apples left on a branch after all the others had been picked tasted especially sweet. They made up for the immature ones in June that had set our teeth on edge.

December lulled me into hibernation, spinning its sleepy time web. The snow came down slowly like confetti, layering the branches with white velvet. And as the trees stored warmth and sap, and the wind blew the remaining crumbled leaves around in big swirls, I moved indoors to activities around the old tiled stove and the nearby kitchen table.

I remember best the summer nights. They would often find me resting my back against the bark of a trunk and hoping that my boyfriend Ernest would soon join me. I had fallen for Ernest with uninhibited feeling but was not yet sure what to do with this new sensation. Sitting under my favorite apple tree I took its pulse. Once I was caught there in a warm drizzle. The bark was singing, and the roots gurgled like underground rivulets. Waves of birds circled the crown, flies droned, and grasshoppers jumped to the rhythm of my heartbeat. Lightning bugs blinked off and on as it got darker. I looked skyward through the dense foliage where throbbing stars were beginning to glisten like insect eyes. I pressed my body into the tree hollow and lifted my face into the spray, letting the soft drops lick my skin with their ticklish tongues. The firmament was silver with moonlight.

Butterflies fluttered through my entire body until I heard Ernest's footsteps bouncing over the cushy grass in my direction. As soon as he stood in front of me all movement stopped, and we were suddenly timid. Ernest gently let himself down next to me. We remained silent. Then the tenseness lifted, and we were close again. We traded stories without pause, as though we would lose the connection between us as if we stopped, even to breathe.

The night air pressed against our eager young bodies, and we were camouflaged by soft darkness. The branches gave us gentle cover. Ernest kissed me under my apple tree and I shivered with a fresh awareness like a quivering green leaf.

Our blissful life changed with the onset of World War II. My father and many other men were drafted and we who were left behind retreated into our close family circles and into ourselves. Ernest was inducted into a German youth group, and looking forward to snuggling together under our apple tree abruptly ended.

Mr. Franz was too old to be drafted. He continued to prune the trees and harvest the apples, which he no longer freely shared with us but sold instead. On a bitter cold January day we heard hacking sounds and saw the first of our beloved trees fall to his axe. In the coming years two more trees shared the same fate. After the felling of the first tree, Mother and I sneaked out before dawn and collected the few logs, branches and wood chips left on the ground. Mr. Franz had stored the rest of the tree safely in his shed before nightfall.

The atmosphere of the war years was gloomy and drab, filled with anxieties. We knitted through long evenings, and my mother taught my sister and me to darn socks and patch torn sweater elbows and legging knees.

One morning Mr. Franz discovered two soldiers asleep side by side like drunks in their worn-out, olive-drab uniforms right under one of the remaining apple trees. Later I overheard him tell Mother that they had pleaded with him, "Please help us with anything you can spare," and he had handed them some apples. "They went away," he grumbled, "like godless beggars."

There was great joy and relief when my father returned home. The war was over but the postwar chaos and its deprivations were about to begin. The destruction all around us was chilling. We continued to struggle for survival. My father was forced to find odd jobs, mostly manual labor. He no longer had a position as a lecturer in mathematics because most universities had only partially reopened their doors. He looked plucked and forlorn.

We had sold everything we could spare. We even tearfully parted with Riva, our faithful breeding dog, a golden retriever. A hunter bought her for a bushel of corn, two sacks of potatoes, several bags of coal and a dozen eggs, which kept us going for only a few weeks. But we got by. Somehow my parents found a way to clothe and feed us and even kept the old tiled oven glowing.

Mr. Franz had not totally forgotten us. In August 1946 he delivered a basket of Paradise Apples to our doorstep in exchange for a knitted sweater, which my mother had managed to piece together from leftover yarn. Our delight knew no bounds, but Mother curbed our appetites. She indulged us each with one apple; the rest were preserved for winter. The four healthiest, roundest specimens were set aside for Christmas. We placed them on a newspaper on a shelf next to the canned cabbage and blackberry marmalade in our cool, damp cellar. There they might shrivel a bit but still be a treat for the holidays.

Whenever I was sent to fetch a tin of rations or bring up some coal, I stopped at the display of apples. I fingered them, running my hand over the wrinkly surfaces, then bringing my nose into smelling range, inhaled the familiar sweet fragrance. Once I lifted the rosiest apple off the shelf only to put it back quickly as if I had been stung. By November only the four special apples decorated our cellar shelf. The rest my mother had used for cooking.

The Advent season is a time of preparation in most German households, filled with baking and the making of presents. One frosty evening when our stomachs growled like hungry hounds, my mother decided to donate her Paradise Apple while we were busy wrapping and gluing tiny golden angels onto gifts, readying them for delivery to family members and friends. She quartered the reddish ball, then we dipped our portion into warm honey. We let that taste linger on our tongues before finally swallowing. Later in bed, Inge and I speculated what might happen at Christmas. We were convinced that Father would share his apple with our mother. He was a very giving man.

I never liked the cellar. Except for a slit of a window at ground level, the cave-like room was dim and musty-smelling. Even on a bright, sunny day little light filtered in. At dusk we used the single light bulb which dangled on a long wire from the cellar ceiling. The steps down to the cavern were worn and rickety. The cellar floor was made of concrete and was slightly slippery from the permanent moisture. Only the sight of our three remaining Paradise Apples lit up my mood every time I was called upon to go down to the cellar and bring something up.

Two weeks before Christmas, unusually cold winter days arrived. At the gold-green haze of twilight my father returned from the woods with firewood and splintered it for kindling. Earlier that morning my mother had come home from the black market with meager exchanges of flour and shriveled potatoes. Once a magician at the stove, her cooking had become uninspired under the burden of the dwindling food supply. This didn't stop us from lying to her every night: "It's so good, Mutti." That night, after a small fire crackled in our tiled oven and a pungent odor of sap and cooking oils circulated through the warm kitchen, she told me to fetch a jar of red cabbage. She was making potato dumplings again. Gingerly, I made my way down the cellar steps and pulled the light cord.

That's when I saw him. As soon as the light blinded us both, he spun away from me, his back rounded into a shield, withdrawing his neck into his frayed jacket like a turtle. I froze in my tracks, dumbfounded. I had only seconds to make a choice. I could have withdrawn inconspicuously, silently retracing my steps back up the stairs. I could have ignored his transgression, saved him the embarrassment. But I had seen the bite, a rosy, dripping wound.

Defiantly, I took a stand and waited until my father decided to face me, hand extended, the forbidden fruit glistening in his cupped palm. Suddenly I stepped forward, a feathery panic in my chest and took the cherished Paradise Apple from him and plunged my teeth into the soft flesh. At that moment innocence changed places with the knowledge of sin. I stood glued to the damp cellar floor. Sharing my father's guilt tasted deliciously sweet.

I can't remember how long we stood there in deep shame, our heads bowed toward each other like top-heavy tree crowns, the quiet broken only by the taps of a tattered twig against the glass of the cellar window, which on that night let no light into the darkness, not even the faintest glimmer of a star.

ROSES FOR MY MOTHER

EVEWLYN LEWIS-CHASE

It was the best of our times, soon to be the worst of mine. There in the back of the backyard is where I remember my father best. The man I knew then was the one I still hold in my heart

Clouds of petals bloomed over my head while I sat, Indian style, under an old gnarled cherry tree, watching and listening as you tended your rose garden.

I hear you now as then: "They aren't mine. I'm a caretaker; roses belong to God." Sometimes you told stories or quoted poetry in storie. "The Cremation of Sam Magee" was a favorite..

I was five when you asked which rose was my favorite and I learned some history. My choice was called "Bess" for a first lady and you told me about Mr. Truman and his general.

Each day you studied long and deliberately before you finally selected and cut one perfect bloom. Then together we took the rose in a bud vase to Mother, who was soon to leave us..

The day she died the roses started to decay and that wonderful closeness we shared seemed to wither, slowly fading. You brought the other too soon and then you planted vegetables in my enchanted garden.

I lost you and it was never the same. I mean I know you can't go home, but we were still there. I never left.

PLATE OF BONES

JAN CHRONISTER

Clouds are fishbones
left on a sky blue plate.
Hummingbirds stop still
in stifling heat to drain
remaining geranium juice

My husband tends corn and tomatoes
feverishly
fighting drought and joblessness.

36

We wait for August to serve us
leftovers from deer and taxes.

MEMORIAL GARDEN

Pam Crow

You worship in the dirt,
on your knees with a trowel
in your hand. You push
seeds into the earth, slowly,
the way hard truths push
into our hearts, take root there,
pressing the walls larger
to let more light in.

You tell me you don't know
any God, but what of this
conversation of flowers?
Bee Balm, Love in the Mist
whisper to lavender and pansies
yearly we return.

Here, too, is what we wish
we could control: aphids black
on the slender necks of roses,
silver gleams where slugs pass
munching the sweetest stems
right down to the ground.

When so many are gone
I think this is the place to be—
dividing, planting,
making room.

38

DAYLILY IN PARADISE

MARCH DARIN

BEE BALM: ITS long stems spiked like crimson flumes on a Kaiser's helmet, streaking past the cracked kitchen window of the cottage. She loved the way it sounded. Beeee baaalmm. Nature's magnet for hummingbirds, their emerald wings flapping like propellers did at Kitty Hawk.

She surveyed her property, almost an acre of crab apple trees, blueberry bushes (two for cross fertilization), strawberry patch, bushes-gone-wild raspberries and her prize perennials. In between the bushes was a grassy field. It sloped on the edges, but sufficed for the kids' badminton court. The remnants of their tree house, a few scruffy boards their dad had salvaged at the town dump, marked the southern edge. To the west was her neighbor's shed, occupied by splintering lobster buoys and the skeleton of a blue Chevy truck. The northern boundary, the one closest to the road, was guarded by an uninhabited suit of armor retrieved years ago at the Montsweag Flea Market. A touch of chivalry in a town where men still slathered on Aqua Velva Saturday nights before they congregated at the Rifle Club. Still, she was grateful. The roadside knight was a great landmark for out-of-town visitors finding their way from the Maine Turnpike.

39

One Sunday some neighbors had visited, bearing a Rose of Sharon bush. Too bad she was never here to see its pink umbrella-like blooms in May. But she took what she could get. They all did. Simple truth was, she and her kids were lucky to be here on vacation as long as they were, given the crazy schedule of summer life guarding jobs and swim meets.

The universe smiled on her in other ways. Like the air fern she had cultivated in her basement college apartment, her perennials seemed to thrive independent of her care. Her garden looked good for only two months' weeding, deadheading, planting, fussing, and intermittent watering from a fickle well, though her well was said to be the deepest in town. She had planted when the kids were too little to complain they were missing their friends who were drifting through air-conditioned malls two hundred miles away in Boston.

The condensed summer season had its own calendar. First bloomed what locals called devil's paintbrush, splotches of fiery orange too quickly extinguished by the blade of a lawn mower. Then rose mallow and coreopsis, with egg-yolk color blooms that drew monarchs and swallowtails and painted ladies. July brought raspberries so ripe a single tap could release them into your sweaty palms.

But it was the daylilies that captivated her. Strictly low maintenance. She had planted them among the ledge rock, glistening with mica mined a century ago by men with no stomach for earning their living from the sea.

She had read there were more than 1,500 varieties, enough to plant a different daylily every day for almost five years. They had sensuous names like Moonlit Caress. Ominous names like Dark Empire. Mary Todd Lincoln even had a daylily named after her—a bold, yellow bloom—small consolation for cradling a dying husband in your arms. Their life span was even shorter than those of the Monarch butterflies that swarmed around the coreopsis. Twenty-four hours, and a daylily would perish.

※

They had met on the day her clutch died. He had pushed her hill-weary Honda past the last incline so she could glide into her yard. She hadn't figured there were so many hills on the way to the beach. Saying good-bye that late afternoon, he squeezed her hand a second too long. He had noticed her many times before, a pretty woman with an easy smile whose slender freckled arms were always in motion. Hauling in groceries from her Ford Taurus. Pulling out brazen weeds trespassing on her daylilies beds. She and her kids—two brunette daughters who looked like her and a younger son who didn't—had traveled here for a decade of summers from their home in a snug Massachusetts mill town. Snug it was, too snug. Most people knew Methuen for the polar fleece made by the town's only remaining textile factory. She knew it for the tug in her chest she felt as an outsider from Illinois and the wife of a prominent state legislator.

That's why she loved coming here, to this relatively undiscovered peninsula that hung off the Michelin's guide like a jagged tooth from Bath. There was something comforting about the constancy of the waves that washed up over Popham Beach. No matter how tired you were from keeping vigil with a teething infant, or varnishing shingles assaulted by wind and sun, you could always count on the waves. Even the pungent scent of low tide, which her daughter had once compared to a dead mouse that was decomposing under her bed, was soothing.

For the past five years, she had come to the cottage with her three kids, but no dark-haired husband in tow. A local man had noticed. A few times, he had stopped his pick-up truck when he saw her in the yard. "You okay?" he'd call out. If the kids were napping, she'd saunter up to his truck, grateful for a few words of adult conservation. Hers was the last house before the pavement ended on Bailey Road. She was usually on her knees, taming unruly purple clematis on a homemade trellis. Or hammering another nail in the rickety front stairs.

Last summer, he was the only customer at the girls' lemonade stand, paying the inflated price of one dollar for the sugary mix in Styrofoam. She liked him for that. She liked him for his burnt copper skin, and the way his blue chamois shirt looked against it. She liked the way he talked about this bit of earth.

Sometimes she was awakened by his motorboat softly chugging in the hour before dawn, when the last of the August meteor showers had fallen into the Atlantic.

She was a puzzle to this man who lived all his life in the small fishing village where the fire chief ran the gas station. Not like the women here who wore polyester pants from Sears and had their hair done every Friday at Wal-Mart. Not like the other women from Sebasco Resort who wore tight pink Nike sweats when they jogged past the golf course where their husbands were playing until cocktail hour.

Last June, her cousin had stayed at the cottage a few days. "I didn't know who the other lady was staying at your place," he confessed one afternoon. "I just knew it wasn't you."

Her heart melted. She became as smitten as a schoolgirl deciphering an ink-stained love note from a writer declaring his allegiance forever, or at least until summer.

A howl from her neighbor's beagle broke into her reverie. What did he say?

"Friday," he repeated. "Would you like to go to supper Friday?" They could drive to Five Islands, grab a burger and beer at the dockside pub.

He was different. Not a poet or professor, lawyer or stock broker or any of the other men pursuing her on match.com.

This man had salt water in his veins. Here was an invitation to be with someone just because he loved what she loved. The way the wind and tides sculpted the beach landscape. The way the waves broke over barnacle-covered rocks like the green glass of a shattering Coke bottle.

The way Fox Island looked at high tide, a grassy castle encircled by a moat of foam.

After dinner, he drove her home in his pickup truck. He lifted her off the front seat and set her down gently on the sandy driveway. He pointed out the Big Dipper, topsy-turvy in the northern sky. And the Milky Way, a foggy trail above their heads that made her remember long-ago campfires. They kissed, gently. His neck smelled of Old Spice and Ivory soap. The next morning, a ruby red daylily fell to earth.

LATE WINTER JOURNEY INTO SPRINGTIME

CARLA A. FELLERS

> Mother Earth is *"that black soil glittering with mica, black hairy roots, and all life that has gone before, broken down into a fragrant sludge of humus. . . . she is the mulch that makes ideas happen."*
>
> Clarissa Pinkola Estés, *Women Who Run With the Wolves*

I OFTEN STOOD at the windows of my third-floor apartment in Omaha, Nebraska, watching the seasons change and imagining how I'd landscape the grounds. In the middle of the 2004 winter, I stared at a near-record accumulation of snow built up like layer upon layer of thick, down comforters. At first, the shroud of white obliterating shrubs, roadside mailboxes, and small cars was magical; the four-foot drift on the balcony and the 10 inches of snow capping the railing, marvelous. At first, the snow mesmerized.

When cloudless days let sunshine radiate to the roof, the underside of the snow melted, and icicles grew from the dripping eaves. Intrigued, I watched the small, pointy shards of ice grow. However, when the spears elongated to meet the snow mounded on the balcony, fascination turned to fear of being imprisoned. Day after day, I looked out at the balcony, which served as my "yard," where I had 20-some flower pots, and where I wished for a plot of my own dirt.

I wanted to be outside, but outside was inhospitable. It was six weeks to spring. Six weeks to the beginning of green. In six weeks, would all this snow be gone? It wasn't the worst snow I've endured, but it was the most confining. Almost 30 inches of snow, drifted by north winds, heaped by blades mounted on the fronts of pickups, shoveled, tramped—too much snow for too long. Sometimes, the urge to grab a trowel and stir soil grew so strong that I was tempted to stick my pots in the microwave to defrost them. Early in March, I could stand the snow no longer. I drove north.

Outside, gusty south winds and a bright sun are slowly shrinking the mountains of snow pushed to the edges of streets and parking lots. A short journey takes me to eternal spring. Inside my destination, the air is humid and infused with rich, earthy warmth. I stop a moment, close my eyes, and breathe in the essence of compost and warm spring rain.

I walk quickly through the first vast room, past the huge three-tiered fountain and the tastefully arranged groupings of expensive patio furniture—to the greenhouse, where I can wander through row upon row of blooming plants and tropical plants and bedding plants that I wish I could take home but I can't because I don't have a back-forty, only a four-by-forty-foot strip of cement suspended 40 feet in the air. The greenhouse—where there's not a flake of snow.

On cement pathways, puddled with spillage from watering tasks, I amble past tables filled with cheery. white-blooming shamrocks; sensual fuchsia; virgin white cyclamen; velvety, deep purple African violets. My mother grew violets in her Oklahoma farmhouse. She pinched off leaves and poked them into dirt to propagate new plants. Sometimes the leaves withered and dried up. Sometimes they formed roots, made new leaves, and grew to bloom. Some forty years later, she still has descendents of those Oklahoma violets blooming in her Idaho living room.

I walk by a table holding a field of geraniums with blooms the size of my fist. White, red, salmon, purple, and fuchsia. And a color and variety I've never seen before in a geranium—yellow, with feathery-fringed petals. However, like all geraniums, when I crush a leaf, a pungent smell lingers on my fingers. It's not pleasant; not offensive, either. It's concentrated freshness—the distillation of grass, elm trees, forsythias, sunshine, and gray-bottomed cumulonimbus clouds. I close my eyes and I am on the farm where I used to live.

As I wonder which geranium I might take home to brighten the last days of winter, a seductive scent drifts by. I follow it to The Potting Area, where two women pack black soil into moss-lined wire frames and poke baby plants around the surfaces. I stop and inhale, savoring the heavy, warm, moist odors, a smell associated with the history of women. Women—connected to the earth since humans were formed from dirt. Women—of ancient civilizations gathering while men hunted. Women—learning to save seeds and stick them back into the ground to grow the things they discovered were good for food.

The aromas also connect through time and space with the black, loamy soil of my own Oklahoma garden from thirty years ago. I remember jamming in a shovel and turning over the first spring spade-full—kneeling down and scooping up a handful—bringing it close to my face—breathing in the complex essence of decayed plants from last year's garden, decomposed manure, moisture captured from the melted winter snows— all mixed together into a life-giving matrix. The cast-off transformed into something new.

I also remember the tough, gumbo clay my mother worked into a garden. She grew up on an Idaho farm—a different soil and climate than northern Oklahoma where she moved in 1955 with my brother and me. Her Oklahoma farm was on top of a shale hill. Shale my father sold to the county to put on roads. Shale grading into the gumbo clay, reluctant to grow anything but Bermuda grass. Gumbo, that contracts during dry spells and cracks open into crevices deep and wide, unfathomable with sticks and un-fillable with water from a hose. The clay was also virtually un-diggable. But Mother was like many Oklahoma gardeners; she persisted even when the soil was like cement.

She dug up an eight-by-fifty foot rectangle of Bermuda grass sod in the backyard with a shovel. Spending many long days on her knees, she plucked the grass rhizomes from the dirt and tossed them into piles to be discarded in a ditch. She kept digging and planting and watering and hoeing and weeding. She mulched and composted. She fertilized with manure from the cow lot. She transformed the garden plot clay into a reasonable facsimile of topsoil. Around apple, cherry, and peach trees— and an apricot grown from a pit saved from her father's tree—she planted dahlias, gladiolas, and lilies. She planted vegetables. What flourished easily in Idaho, she encouraged to survive in hot, dry Oklahoma.

45

Perhaps that's the seductive power of gardening: it dares me to create something out of nothing. Tempts me to plant zinnia seeds under one-quarter inch of moist dirt and watch expectantly for the first green shoots to push up out of the soil. To shovel, hoe, and rake packed dirt into soft loam. To score long furrows for rows of green beans, carrots, and peas. To sow, cultivate, and harvest. Without a real garden, I make do by transplanting pansies and petunias from eight-packs into containers on the balcony. Without a garden, I settle for repotting the philodendron when it becomes root-bound. Without a garden, I, too, become root-bound in a container-like apartment.

I never wear gloves when I ready my balcony containers for planting. I need to feel the earth on my skin as I squeeze little clods into fineness and fluff-up the hard-packed dirt with my fingers. This seems to be a universal need, as women everywhere dig in the dirt. They rake. They plant. "They poke blackened fingers into mucky soil," digging, as

Clarrisa Pinkola Estés says *in Women Who Run with the Wolves*, for ancient ancestors. Perhaps this digging is a response to some vague memory of goddesses from 7000 B.C. whose statues have no feet, as if they were stuck in the dirt, emerging from the earth. Perhaps women are applying that warm foot encircling Earth like a poultice—feeling the medicinal metaphor course into fingers, up through arms, towards the soul.

As I walk by a table of infant verbenas pinched, pruned, and forced into aesthetically pleasing shapes, I glance out a side door. The yard is barren and brown. In the distance, winter-naked trees wave skeletal arms in the wind. Empty plots are still signed with the names of last year's stock. It's too early for this year's selections. The sky is cerulean, though; a different shade of blue than it has been, promising that spring will really come soon, even though the wind is icy. The translucent plastic sheeting that covers the roof and walls of the greenhouse casts an ephemeral, gauzy white light. I can't see the sky above me, but I hear the whipping wind and the snapping, rumbling roof. It sounds like a gathering of grumbling gods.

I miss a real garden, though. When I moved into my apartment several years ago, I gladly gave up summers spent mowing fescue, weeds, and crab grass; falls spent raking up mountains of locust and sycamore leaves; and winters spent shoveling snow off the driveway. I was tired of yard work.

46

Five years later, I've gazed out windows long enough. I've rested enough. It's time to get back to the land.

A wooden bin half-full of potting soil blocks the aisle. I stop and thrust my hand deep into the dirt and squeeze a handful. I look around, feeling guilty, hoping no one sees me. But it feels so good that I don't want to take my hand out. I want to play in it. Pile it up, poke it, smooth it flat, and draw my finger across it to make parallel furrows. Reluctantly, I move away from the bin, brushing the dust from my hand only after I inhale the scent the soil has left behind. I leave the dirt under my fingernails.

I don't want to leave this indoor paradise. The chilly wind still blusters outside. As I walk toward the exit, I think about how living in an apartment restricts the gardener in me. I force myself to forget about what I would grow in a vast yard, concentrating instead on my pots on the balcony and my plants inside the apartment. A big split-leaf philodendron, saved from the reject corner of a nursery, thrives as long as it sits by a south window. A mother-in-law's tongue keeps sending forth long, pointed leaves, not in normal, straightforward fashion upward, but sideways and crooked in rants and raves—it reminds me of me. I keep starting new airplane plants from the babies that grow at the ends of runners on my mother plant. Why, I don't know, because there's no room for more. It's just compelling to snip off a baby and see if it will take root.

Each of my plants has its unique story of connections between places and people, between generations and re-generation: three pots of philodendron are cloned from a plant that lasted fifteen years before it died from over-watering. This was the first plant that graced the home my new husband and I began together in 1987.

The Norfolk pine I inherited when my daughter moved to Chicago thrives if I keep it out of direct sunlight. Tiny plastic angels she hung on its branches one Christmas still dangle there. They make me smile.

When a trailing succulent my friend in Tulsa gave me bore two waxy, ivory pink blossoms last year, I wished our friendship that had faded away over the years would bloom again.

A European parsley plant like my grandmother grew in Idaho survived the winter inside and waits for the time it can return to the balcony.

A vinca vine kept on the unheated, inside landing surprised me early one March with pale lavender blossoms turned toward the window. I marveled at the flowers and decided if the vinca, restricted to an unnatural location, can bloom, then so can I.

It takes only a few minutes after I leave the greenhouse paradise to reach my apartment complex. As I drive past the buildings, I notice that almost every balcony has empty flowerpots lined up, stacked up. This place is full of women waiting for the time when hands can crumble dormant soil to prepare for new plants, an activity that is not merely a mechanical chore. It is also spiritual renewal. According to Estés, the "gardener's function is regeneration. The psyche of a woman must constantly sow, train, and harvest new energy in order to replace what is old and worn out." We apartment dwellers don't have big yards or even little plots of dirt to dig in when our energy is old and worn out. We regenerate with soil in containers. Plastic pots or clay, it matters not. The important thing is to sink our hands into moist dirt and touch Mother Earth.

Whatever "can happen in a garden" says Estés, "can happen to a woman's soul and psyche—too much water, too little water, bugs, heat, storm, flood, invasion, miracles, dying back, coming back, boon, healing." Healing. Freeing the mind. Strengthening the body. Women have known this for centuries—a garden is a place of healing.

I think this is why my mother battled the gumbo clay. She was healing her heartache for her native Idaho. When saucer-sized dahlias bloomed like her mother's, she transcended the miles to her homeland. Parsley, dill, and an apricot tree connected her to a time and place far removed from Oklahoma. She might complain of the backbreaking toil, but she always seemed happy after hoeing the garden. It wasn't something she ever talked about; it was something I sensed, especially now when I remember the profusion of flowers coloring her gray, rocky yard. It is something I'll feel when flowers on the balcony bloom again.

SEPTEMBER NUMBERS

MARY DINGEE FILLMORE

Drought sucks the grass's green into
the powdered earth of our September garden.
Even purple phlox goes lavender
above parched stalks;
currant leaves brown and crumple.

Ten locust trees on the western edge
haven't heard the news; their roots
still drink December's snows.
Their oval leaves, a dozen
or more to a branchlet,
glow greenly on.

Noting the sun's minutely lower
each day at four o'clock, I sip
the numbered hours, counting until
scarlet and gold drench us all.

My father loved the lacy locusts,
the ease of their small leaves flickering
in the lightest breeze,
the shifting shadows cast
on each other or on me, who still finds
him, an old gardener twenty-five years dead,
in every leaf.

HOUSEPLANT

LYNN FITZGERALD

No cherries here or light bark trees with white flowers,
but a great dusty plane tree with huge leaves, bark
peeling from its trunk.

The house is dark, three floors high, a gothic-
looking place more like a church: Corinthian columns, urns with bushes.
The façade a Portland stone, grey as a London day.

50

The soot stains the copper molding a patina
green, verdigris horse heads rest on each rail post,
and the English ivy twines up the steps.

Layers peel from the roof, the rafters
blackened planks like railroad ties
rising into clouds some unknown destination.

The Wellingtons, dust covered until the next rain
no petunias in flowerbeds to arrange or busy
lizzies spilling out of flower boxes to enrage the neighbors.

 She reads:
            Virgil or Ovid, maybe Juvenal, probably Horace.
The house is wrapped in peat like old bones
in Irish bogs, a museum, deserving one of those blue plaques
on its wall

            its garden blooming in mass confusion.

COMPOST

MAUREEN TOLMAN FLANNERY

Humus remains when the best has been used—
petals of a rose, once scented,
now left to decompose,
the core, the pit, the rotten spots,
what was left on the plate or in the pot,
mulch hot with fermenting,
what's spilled or spoiled or past its prime,
overripe fruit, fungus, waste with mold
and slime, bloated bodies of something dead,
what's been alive but could not stay
now fallen to transformative decay,
hay that will not become the cow,
that, even with four stomachs, she cannot digest,
the reject molecules of every form of life.

At some point the dregs of matter—
waste, dung, slag—putrefying,
                purify,
become the very stuff of newness,
that which life begins in.
And there, at that moment, in the garden soil,
in the striving soul, in the course of a beaten-down life,
is the sod-revitalizing god of ground.

Scenes from a Window

Jan Flexon

I sit here watching scenes from a window
The tree looks so lonely without her branches
Two cats across the street are trying to come
Over to my house but the snow is too deep
The black cat I call Elvis sits in the middle of the street
In a spot where the sun has melted some of the snow
And the other cat I call Music Man can't move his paws buried in snow
He just sits there while a car down the street is spinning its wheels
Going nowhere I guess they are stuck now since they dug themselves in
And on the house next door the icicles are hanging like masterpieces
From the corner of the roof maybe I should get the camera take some
pictures
But I continue to sit here and drink my coffee and continue to watch
I write it all down on paper and then crumble it up so that the cat can play
I feel locked up in silence I feel sore from shoveling snow I feel isolated
When will spring be here when will the flowers bloom when can I open the
Windows and breathe fresh air and feel the sun again on my skin
I want to wear my sandals and baggy shorts and a tee shirt
I feel so many things I think I will write them down and make a list

Wrapped up
Layers
Coffee cups
Lover
Hot cold
Snow blow
Time slow
Sunshine
Three below
Wind chill
Time still
Black cat
Cross my heart
Too long
Inside
Screams
No more
Silence

Scenes from a window

WHERE SOMETHING USED TO LIVE

DONNA FRISK

I wasn't ready for this,
this November rain that slaps me
like a wet towel, this wind
that sneaks down my collar
and up my sleeves, this chill
that drills into my bones.

I've put suet out for downy
woodpeckers, flickers, and juncos.
The not-yet-sleepy squirrels
thieve sunflower seeds meant
for chickadees and sparrows.
I feel guilt for the smorgasbord
I've created for a juvenile
Cooper's hawk. So brief

was the sharp smell of summer's end
that lured me out into the last thralls
of my garden, the leaves—yellow,
gold and brown ornaments,
twisting and turning, tenuously
connected, faded flowers bowing
to earth, depositing their seed
upon the ground. Not just summer,
but fall gone, too, an ache
I can't put words to—a hollowness
where something used to live.

THE SERPENT, AGAIN

BARBARA GOLDOWSKY

In Australia, flocks of parrots
die in orchards after feasting on apples.

Here, you tell me paradise isn't forever,
that all beginning shelters within it
an end—a bitter, inescapable pit.

Though you remind me
each love is a death
I am a daughter of Eve.

I will eat of the tree
and expect to get bitten
by snakes.

SALUTE

BARBARA GOLDOWSKY

The grapes are trellised, tied,
and expertly cut back,
the peach espaliered, crucified
against the wall.
The orchard grass is weedless,
one-point-eight-five inches tall.
The tulip field grows upright,
no stem slack.

In the perennial bed, the roses
wait, like Mata Haris staked
for the firing squad.
And nowhere grow untidy posies
of violets or uninvited blooming vine.

No bleeding-heart, this gardener
has drawn the line!
Salute her, in her doomed but brave
attempt to win the border war.

OCTOPUS GARDEN PARADISE

JULEY HARVEY

i feel rich
when i return
from the sea,
as if il've been
willed unexpectedly
an inheritance
from a favorite
fairy godmother,
venus on the half-shell
meets glinda the good witch,
with a bounty saved
in a cedar driftwood treasure chest,
full of funny,
shiny, kelp-gardeny, frond-wavery things
that once had fin or wings.
if you catch the sea
at the right moment, tide, light,
it appears free
of man,
as wildly innocent
a garden as paradise,
a flash
in the peter
pan.

ACHE OF OUR HANDS

JERRY HAUSER

Our hands have passed their strength
among the shrubs and bushes.

Trimmed and thinned their branches.
Worked among the peonies and dahlias.
Tied them firm to the wind.

Worked among the roses and morning glories.
Trellised them that each leaf will take the full sun.
Plant after plant and bush after bush with shears,
coarse twine and slats of wood.

56

And our hands begin to ache,
scuffed and scratched they are with
dirt wedged into the breaks and crevices
of healed-over calluses.

But an ache that satisfies. salutes our staying
on that right though weed- and rock-strewn trail.
The journey is not without the open wounds
that etch their sweet pain into our travel.

But we persevere in spite of them and finally
realize how near we have come to that garden nova–
the exploding light of the lovely dawn that finally
hails, "You have made it! Let me hug you and cover
you with kisses. You and your argosy of flowers
have arrived! And gloriously!"

GARDENER IN THE SNOW

NANCY J. HEGGEM

It's January, Northern Illinois, need I say more?
Mailman adds one more catalog to the well-stuffed box,
not about sheets on sale or the newest electronic gadget.
It's a book of treasures from Misters Jackson & Perkins.
Wow is that Sheer Magic gracing the cover?
Gently I turn the page to meet old friends and new wonders.
There is Welcome Home and a new Lady Bird,
Pope John Paul II, Our Lady of Guadalupe and Diana, Princess of Wales,
Rio Samba, Double Delight and Strike it Rich,
Tahitian Sunset, Wild Blue Yonder and the beautiful fragrant Bella'roma.
The sun's not out; the soil is not running between my fingers.
But my garden is growing; thanks to USPS and 2007 Rose Catalog.

58

IN THE GARDEN

DEANNA HOPPER

AUTUMN: I AM drinking jasmine tea, sweet to the nose, pleasantly bitter on the tongue, drinking tea and looking at the pale yellow leaves of the maple in my front yard. Beside me lies a large glossy book on Japan, open. I have just found the picture of the gate, that traditional Japanese gate with the two top-heavy crossbars, the most massive, topmost one curving upward at the edges, the Torii. I have been trying to remember what the main gate at the San Francisco Japanese Tea Garden looks like. I'm sure this is it. Next, I try to remember what "Torii" means. "Heavenly Gate" or something like that, doesn't it? I look. Here it is. It means "bird perch."

59

I have been trying to recall a moment, one certain moment out of many, which occurred at the Tea Garden. When I try, things that surround the moment fly up from the ground like dry leaves disturbed by a wind, obscuring my object. The Asian Art Museum used to be next door to the garden. I could stroll from museum to garden in a continuous segue; go from looking at bronze Buddhas and slender jade dishes to looking at twisted pines and a moon-shaped bridge, never breaking my mood. Well, the museum has moved to its new digs downtown. That particular gliding segue can't be again.

But still, if I were to go there right now, much would be as it always has been. I would walk up the very wide and shallow steps to the serene massive top-heavy gate, the Torii, which I used to think was called Heavenly. I would pass through. Really, the garden is large, but the bit of it one sees when one first goes in seems so small in proportion to this gate, dwarfed, miniature, charming. There's the centerpiece, the koi pond, twisted and coved and bridged and landscaped and hummocked. I want to touch as well as look at it. I want to stroke the speckled, variously colored, loaf-sized koi drifting, clear but obscured, in the water.

How many times have I been there? Was the first time when I was a child? Was the second time that day with my father? In general, a visit to the Garden goes like this. I enter. Movement on my right catches my eye. I turn to see a little hut tucked into some bamboo. From a tiny dark window protrudes a long stick with a little square basket fastened to the tip. A bit of paper on the side says "$2." The stick jiggles vigorously. Someone, invisible from this angle, animates it. No matter how often I come here, I never remember this. It surprises me every time. I pay, a little sheepishly, and the stick darts inside the window.

I go forward, thinking, usually, about my father. On the other side of the koi pond, up several steps, the teahouse stands serenely above and looking down on the pond, on the moon-shaped bridge, on the heavenly—I mean the bird-perch!—gate.

That "face" of the teahouse, the side facing the garden, so much a part of it yet so above it, seems somehow protective, somehow related to the immutably serene bronze Buddhas of long ago. The teahouse is roofed but not walled, open to the air, and to sit in that spot, the seats looking down on the garden, is inexplicably desirable, irresistibly beckoning. Those seats, however, are taken.

Mounting the steps and entering, I'm walking slowly by those sunlit front seats, glancing bitterly at the people in them, wondering if they are tourists or locals, wondering if they know they are happy. I scan the interior. Quite dark by comparison; no view, either. At the very back of the teahouse, near the kitchen door, one table, as if trying to escape, is at least under the sky, not the roof. I sit there. At my back rises a rough wall of stone and cement. From this spot, much of the larger garden is behind, but also above me, out of sight. At this table, I can lean my head back and look at the sky, which is always changing. I have sat here in sunny weather; I have sat here, in a long wool coat buttoned to my chin, in January (the front seats were still taken). I have sat here so often that I think of it as "my" table. I pour my tea, hot green tea, pleasantly bitter on the tongue, and write in my journal, leaning my head back from time to time to look at the ever-changing sky. Tendril-shaped bits of cloud writhe in the San Francisco sunlight, which is now hazy, now glittering, now milky and chill, now warm and yellow. I am more than satisfied, but I still glance at the front, in case a seat should vacate.

I write in my journal now: *I am pretty sure that my second visit to the Garden was as a fourteen-year-old, with my father. It was after the divorce. Dad was spending the day with me. I don't know where my sister was; she may have made an excuse to get out of the visit. We were both uncomfortable with him. What makes the memory of that visit so strange was an instance of my father's uncanny luck. My poor, disastrous father, who should never have been anyone's father or husband, had this bizarre lucky streak. No matter what he did, no matter how reckless he was, he never went to jail, never went bankrupt, never lost a limb. The only time he was sued (that I know of) he charmed the man suing him into abandoning the suit and forming a business partnership—a business partnership!—together. The newspaper wrote them up and ran the article with a picture of them shaking hands. It was always like this.*

60

The day my father brought me to the Japanese Tea Garden, he led me up the steps in picturesque golden sunlight (already odd, but I didn't know it) and we took a seat facing the garden. I liked it, but I didn't appreciate the singularity of the moment. I thought I would be able to sit there again and again in the years to come, anytime, as often as I felt like it. It never happened again.

We sat there, waiting for our tea to cool, and we were happy. There was nothing to do. The garden and the teahouse were full of birds and people; they all seemed happy, too. The sun seemed unnaturally close, as if it shone only on this one little spot. The light seemed to come from only a foot or two above our heads, yet it didn't bother our eyes. The birds, quite tame, fluttered about for crumbs. One landed, yes, in front of us, between my left hand and my father's right one, on the counter, no further away than the edge of my journal is now. We sat very still. We were looking at this bird, and he was looking at us, when I noticed that his left leg ended at the knee in a tiny smooth knob. He stood there, sleek, even impatient, waiting for his bit of rice cookie. There was no blood. He didn't even lean to the right to compensate for his missing leg. His eyes and feathers glistened as they should. This–with the sun, and the bird, so close–was very brief. We made him wait an instant too long, and he beat the air with his perfect wings and disappeared.

I close my journal, close the book on Japan, and lean back and pour myself another cup of tea. I look again at the pale yellow of the dying leaves.

My father died last year. I heard about it through a cousin, and I shouldn't have been surprised. My father did not die in a car wreck, of a drug overdose, or of liver failure. His body was not found, weeks after the fact, in a filthy, isolated trailer. Against all odds, unbelievably, my father died in a proper clean hospital, with friends to visit him and morphine for the pain.

It puzzles me to think about my father, and about luck, how we wind up with what we get. Was my father's luck any more bizarre than that bird's? How could a bird lose just a leg, anyway? How does a creature so fragile–a bird, or a human being–lose proportionately so much of itself, come so close to death, and yet live? And how, while being so mutilated, could it be so perfect?

The mutilated, perfect bird flew away from us that day, through the always-changing sky, possibly to its perch: that whole massive ritual gate erected to honor a little gray bird with one leg. This is not so much luck as oracle, but there is no priest to interpret it for me.

My father has gone into the land of the archetype. He has joined the bronze Buddhas and the symbolic gate and the inscrutable teahouse gazing down on the pond of drifting koi. . . and I find I feel a wry, watery gladness about that. In spite of everything, I wish him well. This wish is his final bit of uncanny luck.

PRUNING FRUIT TREES

DORY L. HUDSPETH

They say you just keep at it,
cutting off what bends down
or goes out too far from the trunk
to support fruit without breaking.
There's a certain art to subtraction,
a sharp dance around and around.
When you're done you are supposed
to have spaces big enough to throw
a cat through, nice and airy.
But it may depend on the size of your cat.

62

A GARDEN DRESSED FOR EVENING

DORY L. HUDSPETH

Colors, now subdued are
Adorned by a rope of fireflies.
They are splinters of light to accent
The wide deep moonlight.
Shadows arrange themselves neatly,
An elegant black shawl scented with honeysuckle,
Iridescent moonflowers,
Embellished by cricket's refrain.

A WALK THROUGH MY (DIGITAL) GARDEN

GARY JUGERT

YIPPEE'S GARDEN VANISHED. He should have known it would happen in an exclusively electronic world created by eight gajillion megabits of ones and zeros flying willy-nilly about across his liquid crystal display screen. The world rendered in megapixels may look like the world, but it's not the world. It's a frenzied parody of life as we think it should be and its time for Yippee's garden flashed by like an illuminated simulated firefly.

His garden began (and ended) when he logged into The Game yesterday.

Sitting in the basement of his mother's house, Walter Gottfried spent most of his time gazing into a computer screen programming his warrior character to be stronger and healthier than the other combatants scattered worldwide and brought together through the magic of high-speed Internet. He spent every penny he earned from his newspaper delivery job on better armor for his electronic persona, on faster land speeders to whisk him from battle to battle, on more powerful weaponry, and of course on the secret mystical potions to bring him invisibility, super jumping power, and an almost irresistible masculine charm. Inside of The Game, Walter turned into Yippee. Walter, the depressed, anorexic, pimply-faced 40-year-old newspaper boy with agoraphobia ceased to exist and Yippee stood in his place adorned in full armor and with the type of chiseled good real life reserves for others.

63

But yesterday something came over Yippee.

He tired from the battles. The trolls, the goblins, the mean fairies, the vampires, the invisible atom bombs, the endless series of monsters and never-before imagined perils seemed uninspiring. Yippee didn't want to attack and kill anybody yesterday. He wanted to find a nice house, meet a nice girl, start a coffee shop, and maybe give birth to a couple of children. He wanted to hang electronic pictures on electronic walls. He wanted a digital garden. And with his Ultimate Master status, he could easily afford to purchase everything he needed.

Except the girl.

So he'd set out to acquire everything he needed in The Game. He visited the most obscure corners of the synthetic world seeking someplace quiet and serene. He wanted to be on a dirt road, with rolling hills and lots of flowers and trees. He wanted the houses to be other-worldly, but not weird or scientific-looking. He wanted a big plot of land with lots of available data space to plant his garden, and perhaps build a wheelbarrow from the graphic design toolbox under the "create" menu. He wanted nice neighbors who kept their plots nicely adorned even without covenants and an overlord to rule the demesne. An hour after logging on yesterday, he'd purchased an acre of unreal land far away from the centers of battle he'd memorized over the last two years of playing The Game.

He then visited the shops he'd always ridiculed.

He bought furniture and pictures and rugs and a fountain for his front yard and a box with 73 different houses. He rushed to place everything "just so" in his yard. He manipulated the tools to make the area around the house bumpy and make the area by the street flat. He put up a white picket fence. Some of his neighbors stopped by to chat. They all welcomed him to the neighborhood. When those who knew the full details of the warrior codes examined his attire, they asked him if he intended to bring the war to their sleepy simulated burg, but he assured them he'd given up the battle and only wanted to settle down and decorate his new land.

And then he pulled out his most exciting purchase.

The box of plants.

Above Walter's computer screen in the real world, a small dirty window allowed in the afternoon sun. He often sat behind his computer all day long watching his mother's bent shoulders and slow gait work in her garden. She knew how to turn dirt into flowers, and vegetables and bushes and trees. She ambled through her small patch of backyard nirvana bringing life to nothingness. Walter wished he could stand being outside during the daytime because he wanted to know the secrets of water and fertilizer and seed and light. But his mind rebelled whenever he tried. Walter knew too well the life of a vampire. He never felt secure unless the moon and stars watched over him and the sun hid its garish glare.

Yesterday, three hours after logging on, Yippee began the half-day long process of turning a square acre of cyberspace into a lush garden. He placed flowers of every variety in dazzling displays. He planted trees of the most exotic sort throughout his little paradise. He lined up row after row after row of ripe vegetable begging to be plucked by electronic

64

fingers. His tiny cottage burst forth with the most magnificent display of horticultural genius ever displayed in The Game.

As he finished planting a series of climbing red roses along his wooden picket fence near the road, a small girl found her way down the dusty road. She stopped to say hello to Yippee and compliment him on his acreage. She lived down the street, operated a discotheque in the nearby digital city, and lived in Australia in real life. She couldn't believe all he'd done in such a short time.

"Would you like to take a walk through my garden?" he asked the girl.

"Of course!" she said. She'd never seen anybody spend so much money on plants anywhere in The Game.

As they strolled about and Yippee described his future plans for his yard, his pride of ownership oozed through the instant message chat box. He obviously loved his new house. Somewhere in Australia, a woman smiled as she extended a crooked index finger to the F5 button. Suddenly, the tiny little girl who came free with the neighborhood grew to be 26 feet tall, wearing full armor, and brandishing the most horrifying of all the weapons created in The Game. She owned a Neighborhood Blaster.

"I find you here, you despicable weasel!" screamed the giant woman as her cannon began to blast every building in sight. Yippee's garden roasted instantly under the siege of fire. He raced to pull weapons and armor from his inventory to protect himself from her wrath. He realized too late the evil woman destroying this distant corner of The Game was the woman he'd been fighting for years. He didn't even know if she was a woman in real life or not; he just knew he'd never vanquished her despite battle after battle. He didn't think she'd find him out here in the sticks, and yet he should have known. Her power and her anger at the things he'd done to her over the years should have led him to realize nobody could be trusted on a walk through his garden. He'd spent all day building a miniature paradise and with a few seconds of strategic typing, she'd leveled the entire region and brought strife and chaos into the imagined lives of people who didn't want to play The Game for its combat features.

Many of the residents who'd greeted him warmly a few hours earlier came to pelt him with stones as they watched their electronic creations leveled by a giant they'd never met. Many began sending instant messages to The Game designers to complain about two Ultimate Masters wrecking their creations.

By the time Yippee armed himself and chased the woman away, his property and all the other properties appeared as if a cyclone had

65

landed and spun the entire neighborhood into rubble. It would take days of effort by everyone to cure the mess. Even then, Yippee knew he'd never be welcome in this neighborhood and he also knew she'd be back to wreak the same havoc again. He needed to return to battle and leave the tiny village where he'd been so happy. He needed to give up gardening. It hurt too many lives.

Somewhere in real life Walter sighed.

He wanted to go out in the light and plant something beautiful, but the ever-present danger of giant women from Australia loomed darkly on his heart. He would remain seated and seek them out with the purpose of destroying them and hopefully end their lives before 3 a.m. when he would need to leave to deliver the morning news. He wouldn't garden anymore; it was just too dangerous.

THE BEE

BOBBI DYKEMA KATSANIS

I burn to fling my body into banks of flowers,
to writhe deliciously in erotic scents,
to smell with skin, and taste with flesh,
rub feet with stamens in ecstatic dance.
The hive is sweet, my love, as sweet as fire
that pushes green shoots upward towards the sun.
Fire both from heaven and from under earth
where roots are seen, desire is colored green.
The bright bush beckons.
I am all aflame.

GARDEN DELIGHT

MARIE LOGGIA-KEE

I lay back in bed
Gazing upon overgrown grass
   and spirituous weeds
      and grow a little garden
         within my womb

To dig deep within the dirt
through the top layer
   of warm dryness,
      plunging
 down
   further
until my fingers touch
     swollen lips

Small seedling starts
sprouting its way toward
      the sun

As a baby grows within

68

I PASS OVER YOU

ZOE KEITHLEY

1.   In the garden, I pass over,
touch the way the cry of a bird
touches the hills. I am
that bird, circling, crying.

2.   My veils are ochre,
sequined with mother of pearl.
I am the harvest. Still,
I enter the body of your flesh
as rain enters the earth,
and finds its salvation.

3.   You open your ribcage,
show me strings of jewels.
 I touch them with my fingertips,
and exquisite sounds search me.
Then, in a passion of requite,
I reach down and open my breast;
but slowly, so you can stand the light.

4.   Here on this earth
I am a small brown wren
of subtle markings.
I fly close to home.
Where you are,
I am white-feathered,
of strong wings.
We travel far.

70

HOMECOMING

AMBER KEMPPAINEN

HIGH IN THE mountains, just underneath the clinging folds of perpetual fog, a small girl stared forlornly out her bedroom window. Only it wasn't really *her* window; being an orphan meant nothing was really hers. Miss Diane told her and all the orphans to believe that someone out there was looking for someone just like them. But each day came and others left with new parents, going to homes of their very own. And each day ended with one less friend and dwindling hope. No one ever looked twice at the skinny girl with the strange golden-green hair. But Lily couldn't help wishing for something of her own–a place that was just for her.

As she watched the sun disappearing behind the mountains, single tears welled up in her bright blue eyes and drifted down her cheeks. She folded her arms on the windowsill and tilted her head, trying to see the first star as it appeared, but her gaze was drawn to the tree on the hill instead. Its dark green leaves were black against the evening sky. The pale blossoms of every size and color filled the air with such an incredible smell, like cotton candy, bubble gum and vanilla all mixed together. When she was sad, the wind blowing down the hill brought the scent from the flowers and the sound of leaves rustling in the breeze and it made her feel a little better. And so like every night, Lily wished she could find a way into the walled garden to get closer to the tree.

Access to the garden didn't used to be restricted. Miss Diane said that a long time ago, the garden was a place where the entire village would go to have picnics. The adults would sit in the shade of the big trees and watch their children splash in little pools of spring fed water. It always sounded so wonderful, but she didn't know why it was closed now. The boys at the orphanage told her there were plants in the garden that liked to eat little girls. Venus-People Traps, they'd said, trying to scare her. They said people built the wall so the plants couldn't creep out at night and steal kids from their beds.

Even the older people who volunteered at the orphanage wouldn't tell her anything at all. They remained quiet when she asked, acting like they didn't think she was old enough to know. Lily scowled. *All they tell me is to stay away.* But as long as she could remember, she had felt the garden calling to her. Sometimes it was almost as if, if she could just listen a little harder, she would be able to hear the exact words it was saying. But even if she couldn't understand them, she knew she had to get inside–that all her questions would be answered if she could just find a way in.

As she watched the fog rolling in off the mountains and into the village, she felt a quiver of excitement. Tonight was the night she would get inside the garden, she just knew it. Miss Diane never bothered her after an adoption–she knew Lily needed some time alone. But still, she felt a little bad as she sneaked out her bedroom window and into the blanket of mist. Everyone she asked had warned her to stay away from the garden, but she couldn't. She felt a little shiver run down her spine as she hurried up the hill and the sky grew steadily darker.

Lily was breathing hard as she reached the top of the hill. Taking deep breaths, she picked up a stick and poked at the wall surrounding the garden, searching for a way in just as she had on other nights. Her pale blue eyes narrowed speculatively, as she stared at the slick stone wall covered with dead, twisting vines. She couldn't go over the top. She knew from experience that the walls made her hands hurt and they were too slippery and smooth to get a good grip. The thick vines that covered the outside surface were dead and so fragile they broke at the slightest touch. Lily felt terrible about hurting them more.

If she couldn't go over, she was going to have to go through. Her skin prickled as though someone was watching her through the tiny holes she found in the wall. She knew that someone was already inside just waiting for her to find a way in. But it was foolish to think that. The garden that lay behind the wall belonged to no one in the village–no one would tend it. Only when the branches and vines swarmed over the top of the stone walls did anyone take an interest. Then, it was only the power company–spraying the walls and the vines so the branches wouldn't grow up and into the wires. Those were the worst days–days when Lily always swore she heard screaming from the garden.

Lily jumped as her stick brushed over a patch of vines and she felt them give a little as though the stone behind them was broken or cracked. Pushing tentatively, the old vines parted easily, showing her a crack just big enough for a seven-year-old, or a very small eight-year-old. Looking over her shoulder to the village she'd left, she felt a little guilty as she pushed the vines aside, but rebelliously dispelled the feeling.

There was nothing back there for her, for a girl who had never fit in. Nothing for an orphan no one wanted. Now that she had found a way

72

in, there would be no turning back. Lily peered at the crack, it was a narrow passage, but a nearby street light illuminated the garden so she could see light all the way through. Moving carefully, she squeezed through the crack, her skin burning wherever she touched the black stone. Halfway through, for one horrible moment, she thought she was stuck, but her determined wiggles sent her sprawling into the garden.

Lily pushed herself to her feet and gasped in amazement. She had imagined a wild jungle–a place for adventures and secret picnics with friends, but this was beyond anything she could have imagined. Her eyes darted frantically, trying to take in everything at once: the shadowy paths, the creeping ivy, and the tangles of flowers she didn't even recognize. The flowers were of every shape and color and vines coiling in spirals along the paths. And the strange thing was, they all seemed to be trying to get closer. Lily looked down as something tugged on her shoes. Vines were twisting around her legs like a kitten. She giggled as a few leaves tickled her chin.

"That's enough; don't frighten the poor child." A warm chuckle colored the air rosy from her laughter. The vines untwisted themselves from Lily and crept across the ground toward the woman, rising to touch her. She watched as the lady spent a moment with each of the plants, touching a leaf here, a branch there or a cluster of buds. As the lady turned her warm smile on Lily, she caught herself grinning, any nervousness washing away as if it had never existed. The lady was so lovely and nice. Her skin was a deep creamy color, her hair a deep rich black and she wore a wreath of the flowers from the tree that Lily loved so much. Thinking of it, she turned to look, but could not find it in the gathering darkness. Lily frowned; it should be just there...

73

"I hope my children didn't scare you," the woman said, drawing her attention back. "They haven't seen a new face here for so long; you must excuse them if they got a little over excited."

"I wasn't frightened," Lily said truthfully. "I knew they weren't going to eat me."

"Eat you?" The lady looked taken aback by her answer. The plants themselves moved away abruptly as though mortally insulted, their leaves rustling angrily. "Why would you think such a thing?"

Lily took a step back, rubbing her arms as the air turned colder. The woman frowned, staring at her arms, seeing the scrapes from the rock wall that still burned slightly. She moved closer, touching the marks briefly and Lily immediately felt soothed by the contact. Bending down to look directly in her eyes, the woman's gaze softened and she tenderly brushed a stray lock of hair back behind Lily's ear. "Come, let's clean these scratches."

This woman seemed so comforting that Lily took her hand without hesitation. Out of the corner of her eyes, Lily could see plants moving alongside them. They were no longer angry it seemed, merely curious and they were all trying to get a better look at her. Unexpectedly she blushed, looking down at her toes. She had never been the subject of so much attention. The woman pulled her closer, as if she sensed her unease. "A little privacy please," she said softly and a thick hedge sprouted around them, shielding Lily from most of the plants, although she could still see a few blossoms stretching to peek over the top.

One stern look from the woman sent the curious flowers ducking behind the hedge. Smiling softly, she gently guided Lily to a seat next to a small pool of clear water. Soft green lily pads floated serenely on the surface. Scooping a small bowl of water, the woman washed Lily's hands and arms, careful not to let a single drop fall back into the pool. The cool water soothed the burning on her skin.

"There now, that seems a little better." The woman patted her arms dry with a section of her dress, the fabric as soft as velvet. She pulled Lily up on her lap, wiping a smudge of dirt off her cheek. "Can you tell me now, why would you think any plant would eat you?"

Stopping only once for a drink from the clear pool, Lily told her everything: about the orphanage and the boys' stories, about Miss Diane and the old people's warnings. She talked until she ran out of words and she lay sleepily against the lady, her head tucked underneath the woman's chin. Sleepily, Lily reached out a hand and gently touched the woman's dark hair. Staring at it in the moonlight, she realized that her hair wasn't black at all, but a deep, rich green. Strangely, this didn't upset her in the least and when the woman dropped a kiss onto the top of her head, Lily smiled and snuggled closer, feeling safe, secure and loved.

Eden was thoughtful as she watched the sleeping child in her arms. Her heart ached; it had been so long since she had held such a young one. Their walls had seen to that. She glared at the black monstrosity with hatred. She had fought the wall for years, digging at the footings; the poison that coated the blocks draining her strength. The child's tale disturbed her. They had no idea what they were doing to her, or to her children.

How many more children waited on the other side, willing, but unable to pass through the walls? How many were left, unwanted, unappreciated? How many suffered from the poison they sprayed? Lily shifted in her sleep, drawing a misty smile from Eden. Cuddling her close, she kissed her golden head again. No matter, here was proof that there was some hope-that her work was not in vain. If one could make it through, so could the others: all it would take was time.

Eden smiled as she laid the sleeping child gently in the freshly turned soil. Another one of her children had come home. She placed the rich, dark soil around her as a mother would snuggle a baby in their favorite blanket. Lily sighed, a soft smile on her lips as she burrowed deeper into the soil. Eden smiled as the child began to bloom before her eyes, her body finding the right nourishment at last. In the morning, there would be a lovely golden bush here with bright blue flowers exactly the color of the sea.

She smiled and stretched, her fingers brushing the curious leaves of the trailing vines. "Let her sleep," she whispered, touching the leaves gently. "Your sister will be ready to play tomorrow night." All around the garden, leaves quivered with excitement. She smiled and stroked and soothed them all, watching happily as they turned and frolicked amongst the walls, echoes of little girl laughter filling the air.

Settling her feet deep within the soil, she reached out to the sky and resumed her true form. Her smooth skin became pale creamy bark, her hair lengthened and flowed along branches to form deep green leaves and sprouted a multitude of sweet-smelling flowers. Seeking her friend West Wind, she sent out her call to her other seedlings-wondering where they had fallen; sending them her love and her scent in the hopes that someday they, too, would find their way home.

SPINACH

ELIZABETH KERLIKOWSKE

Straight-legged and in full green
the seedlings crowd each other in the row.

Perhaps in our mulch enthusiasm
we planted them too close together.

We want each one to have a fighting chance
but as they march toward summer
it's clear—some soldiers must go.

We bend over them as we make the life
or death decisions based on what?

The size of basal leaves? The volunteers?
How embedded the seedlings are?

Who can predict which ones would have
flourished and which would wilt?

No do-overs. We can't bring them back
once they've been plucked from duty.
We can only invest in what's left.

All along the row, decisions whose
results we won't know for months.

That not all of them will make it is a given.

Did we leave the best ones dead along
the road or still living in the trenches?

Sweet Autumn Clematis

Kathleen Kirk

I had not known myself until the fall
when I was hushed, and silver, and sweet.

Everywhere I rose unknown
into the soft air. Even you breathed me

and let me go.
In summer I'll be lavender blue again.

Neither one of us will notice what we have
until it is almost gone

and taking everything with it along the fence,
the way clouds brush away

the moon in the evident sky,
the way a song lingers, yearning for reprise.

78

KEEPING THE FAITH

HOLLY LEIGH

CHARLIE KNEELS ON 81-year-old arthritic knees; pruning shears in hand, snipping at a 50-year-old bush rampaging across his front lawn.

"Here, this woody nub," points his wife, Libby, of nearly that long, "and this knob, and this one," as she grabs at the intricate wooden stick maze of the overgrown greenery.

"This was once a mere climbing vine going up the lamppost," she gestures as she eases herself onto a strategically placed lawn chair. "We've always had a lamppost."

"We planted all these trees and shrubs 30 and 40 years back," adds Charlie between snips. "Called Corliss," he continues (the expensive local nursery Charlie had advised me to forsake). "We know the Corliss son well." He repeats this information for emphasis.

"Yep, we know the son and he came right over and helped plant everything."

I hope to stay off topic about my slash pruning of the matching azalea in my yard next door. I had heard how they had planted the bushes jointly with Walter, the long retired Polish man whose house I had bought last fall.

"Your cherry tree has shriveled leaves; bugs you know," Charlie says, his eyes peering into the woody thicket. "You need a spray."

"Ah, Walt planted that cherry tree for Barbara," interrupts Libby. I squint in the direction of the diseased cherry rooted in the memory of a long-dead schoolteacher, Walt's wife. She must have liked white, as I will watch white roses, the two giant white azaleas and white hydrangea resurrect themselves in season. Her ghostly presence lingers.

A few months after I had moved into the brown bungalow that Walter had occupied for 40-odd years and he had moved in with his daughter one town over, neighbors told me that he came in from a walk, hung up his coat, sat down in a chair and drew his final breath.

I grapple with the strange weight of acknowledging people I do not know but whose space and place I have inherited. Spirit of place speaks to me. I realize the front door blowing open several nights in a row coincided with the time of Walt's passing. This makes me shiver slightly in the sun.

"Saw three moose," said Charlie. He is speaking about their weekend road trip to New Hampshire. Charlie's 91-year-old cousin drove them up and down the Kankamangus Highway.

"And we had peach cobbler, "added Libby. I suspect these people are indestructible.

After living in an urban setting for the last 12 years, I am eager for a yard, plants, tasteful lawn ornaments, but it is still too cool for planting.

"Never put in anything in the dirt before June 6," Charlie has warned me. Out of frustration I purchase a green gazing ball. This is New England. It occurs to me that I have lived only in towns inherited from the English and named Greenwich, Yorktown, Cambridge, and now Ipswich.

I recall a trip to England in June where roses the size of dinner plates burst their extravagance in perfectly coifed back yard gardens. A shorter season translated into grander blooms. A transplanted friend speaks to the obsession there about a TV show doing stealth garden makeovers for unsuspecting homeowners. I dream of privet hedges.

80

Plants appear in my driveway or on the front steps. A woman I know from the barn where I ride leaves me a lupine and some border sedum. My postmistress leaves heirloom tomatoes by my side door. Someone was throwing them out and she had heard (from Libby) that I might put in a vegetable plot.

"I don't know what you'll get," Cathy says when I thank her. I like the idea of the word "plot" and all the mystery it implies.

Charlie has ordained that his longtime pal, Buddy, will come cut my grass over the summer and plow my driveway come winter. I find Buddy and the neighbors congregated in the road in front of my house one afternoon. Stan and his wife hold beers in foam sweat holders. The untamed corner lot and growth that runs on my side of the street seem to be the topic of conversation.

"Walt kept the hedge this side along the street real trim," mentions my neighbor with all the snowmobiles and pickup trucks parked in the road across from me. Buddy twitches and nods. They have all known each other forever. More remarks, swallows, nods toward the broken red picket fence. The three reminisce about the 90-plus woman in the faded peeling red house with the wood sunbursts carved over doorways. The lot is actually her property, but the shrubbery is on my line. I get the hint.

I have entered the gardening wars. I stuff my window boxes with red geraniums and small cascades of alyssum the way Walter had done. Red does look best against the brown shingles. That impressed me when I first saw the house. I only add dusty miller to the mix. I accumulate a few gardening tools to store in the barren shed.

"Legend has it," a woman at the deli informs me, "that when the Old Man of the Mountain falls off, there will be no summer." New Hampshire's stone-face icon had slid off unseen during a foggy night. And during the long late wet spring I start believing in this newly minted myth.

After the window boxes, I am at a loss over how to proceed. I secretly bless Walter for the army of hostas on one side of the house, a long line of orange lilies that appears and the Rose of Sharon pruned into tree sculptures that will sprout large purple blossoms down my driveway in August.

But I need experienced hands to help whip two side beds and the vegetable area into grandeur. My good friend Lorraine, who I call Quiche, drives up from New York with her 11-year-old son Jack in tow. Though she suffers from asthma and is allergic to almost all flora, Lorraine digs right in turning the dirt with a hoe and her bare hands.

We wander the crowded tables of choices at the local nursery. After loading bags of mulch, we cart purple salvia, orange mums, Shasta daisies and two foxgloves to anchor the corners of the beds. We select forget-me-nots, pink pewter dead nettle and lavender for the herb strip beside the mossy bricks by the back steps. In go marigolds, basil, sage and rosemary to join the tomatoes.

And the flower that always spoke country and summer to me: blue morning glories. I remembered blue glories' trumpets wrapped on fence posts on visits to relatives' farms in North Carolina, the hum of summer insects filling the air and a rusted chain-link fence decorated with blue flowers in a neighbor's yard. We buy two pots with two-foot green vines. Jack throws up the ball of twine across the roof portico of my side door. Quiche secures the twine in reach of the vines buried on either side of the red door. Trained on twine, my own bower will grow racing its tendrils up to embrace the others in a green snaky cloud.

At night, when the moon slides from one side of the sky to beam its bluish hue in another window, I sense the things growing and alive outside. Crickets and insects speak; wind tinkles in the chimes. I listen for the rhythm of rain on the roof. Each day, I watch the sky and grasp my plots' needs for water, fertilizers and. deadheading. I notice the glints of beetles and the tiny shiny ants that traverse the bride walkway. When

I leave town for a week, worried about the heat, the garden prospers. All the colors and blooms look more robust.

But something is snacking on the lower morning glory leaves. Slugs say the neighbors, so I pour an entire Corona into a tin to lure the assailant. In the morning, the turned over tin has been siphoned clean. Too much for snails. I have served some other guest.

I try to hire an old-hand gardener to trim my perimeter hedges that have gone wild and to prune back the wall of roses pushing into the driveway. I also plan to put in a holly bush.

But week after week he puts me off, "because of the bugs," he says when I stop by the nursery. True enough, I live close to the Ipswich River and tidal marshes that hatch mosquitoes en masse, but this man who works in landscaping baffles me.

I sense an undercurrent that my neighbors on all sides are critical about my unruly shrubs. I hear it in the praise for the guy clearing and contouring his back lot in my view.

I now feel self-conscious pulling into my driveway, careful not to bump the roses.

After sipping lemonade on the porch looking out at the hairy hemlocks and wild tangles of the forsythia hedge, I know I must take these overgrown matters in hand. I buy a trimmer and start giving power haircuts. I lean into the sturdy azalea to even her shape.

I hack maples sprouting up everywhere. Fronds litter my wake; I sweat, snarled in the roadside rose prickers.

By late August, the tomatoes are growing ripe; cherries and yellow pear shapes hang like ornaments. Basil, destined for pesto, rosemary and sage stand knee-high. More donated specimens appear: a lily-of-the-valley and columbine that blooms right away though it is supposed to be a spring flower. Since I had never seen a columbine before, I welcome the purple and white faces. They back up white roses that Walter left behind. Alyssum seeds blown into cracks in the drive bloom tufts of white in the asphalt.

Seated on folding chairs in the driveway in front of their garage, Charlie and Libby are sorting tools and singing in soft voices to each other. The lyrics to "Love and Marriage" drift over the supported lilac that separates our yards. When Charlie sees my basket filled with my first tomatoes, he offers me a cold can of beer on this sweltering afternoon.

"Walt and I always bet a beer on whose tomatoes would be first," he tells me. I sit and admire the giant red-gold coleus border by their garage and this couple's longevity.

I cannot help but notice the boat they are now too old to operate; it is lovingly stored inside.

Later, I will hear tales of water-skiing on the river, clams on the grill, Charlie ice-skating on the river with neighborhood children, the grand times had here on Grant Court. They have lived here for 50 years. Libby's grandfather built both our houses, matching brown bungalows. By Halloween though, they have secured their shrubs with twine and have packed up their white Ford for the haul to Florida. For the last dozen years, they have traded New England winters for a balmier climate.

By November, the holly bush is in place, her red berries festive. By December, surrounded by white snow and silence, the temperatures drop below 10 degrees for days on end. Animal tracks crisscross the tundra of my yard. I make myself imagine the majesty of sunflowers; vivid coneflowers and the black magic ground cover I covet for select spots.

In the corner of the backyard, the green-hued gazing ball stands shiny even in the desolate gray days. I hope to track down a story I heard about a gazing ball offering a portal into the afterlife. Charlie had told me about a white skunk he had spied from his window digging for grubs like a spectral nocturnal ghost. I believe the spirits keep busy.

In January, ice coating the yard has achieved glacial thickness. When the air hits a high of eight degrees, I stand muffled in layers of clothes, scraping my cranky car, when a neighbor pulls up with news. Charlie has passed on in Florida. This is how we vanish. No more tomato contests, summer days and cans of cold beer. I shiver looking at the frozen garden. We believe we are perennial. But the big picture, the cosmos, consists of living, tending, dying. I am still acquainting myself with the terms of timing.

83

It is hard to know what, if anything, remains rooted in a place but auras persist. I note Walt's presence whenever I encounter his wacky wiring spliced all through my house and in the three spider plants he left hanging on the enclosed porch. When the cherry tree he planted for his wife blooms and each time the white roses come back to life, I will pause to think of people I never knew. But I feel the weight of links; the legacy of lived lives, breaking.

On my way home, I stop at the nursery. Rows and rows of lavish photos on cardboard boxes show bulbs in bloom. Crocus, daffodils, hyacinth, tulips. My eyes feast on the rich palette of colors and the exquisite variations on petal shapes. Once planted, faith rises unaided from these plain brown nuggets buried in the earth.

CULTIVATED CONSCIOUSNESS

JENNIFER LEMMING

A natural spring
on my plot
has been tapped,
and pumped. Some parts
of the stream bed
hollowed out,
the bottom made deeper.

84

A bend cut out
to stop erosion, plants
along the bank
evaluated and pruned
if necessary. Rocks brought in
and strategically placed.
My will imposed
on natural processes.

When the rain is plenty,
the white-capped waters
of my subconscious
course down this garden
stream, breaking over
the backs of rocks
that have no subtlety.

WHAT REMAINS

NANCY TUPPER LING

Brunner's heart-shaped leaves
tell you it's time to don your torn
blue jacket; time to spread the lime
over a thawing land.

This year you'll start again
to loosen dirt and worms,
to toss one muddied worn rock
after another into the barrow
like the boy who skimmed stones on Lake Archer.
When the loam is smooth and supple,
you'll raise up the mounds;
each seed fingered from your pocket,
concealed by earth.

Lately you've buried your friends,
passed away like casings
taken by the wind.
But there's something in the weeding,
isn't there—the hot ache of sun?
Some kind of consolation in life
turned abundant under your hoe.

HOME GARDENING

JEROME LONG

As Candide cultivates his garden,
a shrub of rosemary here,
a sprig of thyme there,
Cunegonde plants tomatoes for canning,
potatoes to outlast long winter's fast.
Pangloss arranges legumes
according to their learnéd Latin names.

On an adjacent plot, an adventure-bound
Noah binds broad planks to sturdy beams.
He calls: Forget that stupid garden plot
you've got. Come, see the world. Be a polyglot.

Candide replies: We've been through
enough disasters. For years we toughed
it out. Been tortured in exotic places. Still,
we survived. Here we take comfort, countrystyle.

Cunegonde: I work my butt off in this garden
so I won't have to go begging for food.
Find myself starving again? No deal!
I'll stick to veggies and a home-cooked meal.

Weary Pangloss, pondering what purpose
lies behind the evil besetting man,
concludes: It must be for the best
if we find goodness, here, at last.

In the Garden of Carnivorous Plants

CHRISTINA LOVIN

Even in this dark they writhe there as they did in light
thrown slant against disheveled beds: curious garden
of consuming snare, male and female grown wild: fiber
of fiber, bone of no bone: rouge-kissed mouths
pursed open: soft lipped pitchers pouring in, not out,
and florid staffs, erect and veined as flesh, that rise
above the spread of flytraps' fringe and flange
to guard those gaping gates that once one enters,
none may emerge, but only deep and deeper delve
into that secret, sweet, and drunken death.

Was it not with joy we entered, inebriated by the lure
of hope atremble in our chests like wings of blue-black
wasps, shuddering with delight at sight and scent
drawn out from passion's yawning throat? Our bites and stings
grew futile in the struggle, as we slipped down and down
until there was no longer down or up, but only tall
green walls of light in day and in the night the throb
and tick of outworn wings as struggles ceased, until
our liquefied remains had been absorbed, drawn down
into absolving soil, our bitter carapaces hollowed, dry.

BARE ROOT

GLENNA LUSCHEI

These are unprotected sticks.
Not one leaf. I choose wisteria
to climb the oak,
life up hearty root stock
from the peat moss.

It's bare root season.
In this strange land
I yearn for the canopy
of foliage,
yearn for my old home.

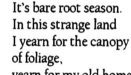

88

Metamorphosis will come for me,
trans-movement through the light.
I will take hold, one day wear
the laurel. I dig, and learn
that I can tether; quick pain
is part of nature.

HOPE SPRINGS

MARIANNE MANSFIELD

DUSK SETTLES OVER the back yard where I sit on my porch step. There is dirt in every exposed crevice of my body, and it feels good. Damned good. I admire my garden and the fruits of my day's labor in it. It looks good. Damned good.

The mud I have scooped up by hand and squeezed into brown clods has allowed me to judge the acidity of my garden soil based on how it hangs together. That same soil, amended with a mixture of organic, non-toxic, high-potency nutrients concocted to counteract any shortcomings, has been hand-cultivated to a depth of exactly six inches. I even used my freshly purchased Shovel that No-Serious-Gardener-Can-Do-Without. What a dandy tool. Contours have been leveled where needed and built up where they were leveled the year before in search of the ideal drainage pattern to avoid those dastardly pools of standing water.

Spring brings with it a conviction that courses through my veins, and today faith surges within me. Everything will turn out as planted. The shrubs and flowers will grow to the height predicted, in the colors promised and bloom at the time of year specified by the tags that have beckoned me seductively from their pots arranged in beguiling rows at the local nursery. The color schemes will mesh with a harmony that will bring peace to any soul, a tear to the eyes of most. In short it will be a masterpiece of beauty, synchronization and tranquility.

My plants are my friends and I treat them to the respect they deserve. We commune. We dialog. We never discuss politics. I once pruned a rhododendron to the size of a pansy during a presidential election year. I apologized to it each day for weeks thereafter, but it never rose again to its former glory. Now I stick to offers of encouragement with a healthy dose of pleading mixed in. This morning as I dug holes just deep enough for their tender little root balls and tamped my pretties gently into place, I urged them forward into summer.

"Please, please, remember that you are billed to be disease-resistant, unappetizing to small animals and impervious to drought. If I have somewhat misjudged the amount of sun that will shine on you by placing you here, buck up! It's sun. It's supposed to be good for you. I've done my part. Now do yours. Please. Pretty. Please."

And there will come a time, an altogether far too brief period of time, when my garden will hint at performing as I have imagined it. Little leaf tips will peek their delicate heads up from beneath the outrageously expensive mulch I have lovingly spread to a depth of precisely three inches. Each day will bring new and more promising discoveries. Look, there are the crocus hybridus. Won't they be divine next to the heliotropium arborescens? (For, you see, this is the season I have vowed to refer to my lovelies by their botanical names only.) And there, there. See the tulipia bakeri? Worth every penny, including the special shipping charge.

We are still weeks away from the dregs of summer when weeds will once again have declared victory in our annual battle for supremacy over my once-pristine flowerbeds. Because I have failed to yank out every one of them by their innocent looking little rootlets, they will have survived to tumble headlong, blown about by that occasional summer breath of air, to land and gain evil foothold under the black-eyed Susans, wriggling themselves vindictively in between the painted daisies, and completely overwhelming the once proud pink dahlias.

90

A day, or maybe two of forgotten watering will have resulted in plants whose once lushly gorgeous flower heads droop sadly earthward. Those that survive will have bolted headlong to grossly ugly seed, being certain in their little plant brains that I, their garden mother, have abandoned them. They will have concluded that it is their fate to disappear forever from the face of the earth unless they get about the business of far-flung propagation at once.

There will be aphids on the roses, and tomato worms will cling menacingly to the Roma vines. They are creatures so disgustingly grotesque I can scarcely look at them, let alone peel them free and send them to their kerosene-filled buckets of death. Alas, farewell homemade salsa. The Japanese beetles will have bored holes the size of quarters through the leaves of the bee balm and Chinese lanterns, despite the army of green and yellow traps positioned in strategic formation throughout the yard. Stunningly arranged bouquets of dried flowers from my very own garden for the Thanksgiving table? Not this year.

In short, it will be time to admit defeat, again, and to begin planning for next year.

But at this moment, on this bright day in mid-May, hope still prevails. It is a hope akin to the hope that buoys along the belief that I can still lose five pounds by Friday in time for my high school reunion, or that I may yet be able to teach myself to play the guitar. It is the hope that anything is possible.

And so, as I perch on my back step and marvel at how cleverly this has all come together, I picture a redwood trellis of bougainvillea set fetchingly between the iris xiphium and the papaver nudicaule. It could be just the perfect exclamation point to the otherwise nearly perfect statement my garden already makes.

That's the thing about gardening. There's always hope for tomorrow.

GERTRUDE STEIN'S GARDEN

LYLANNE MUSSELMAN

A rose is a rose is a rose is a rose
—Gertrude Stein

Gertrude Stein's rockin' rose garden
has no rocks, rocks with roses,
climbing roses, cabbage roses, fragrant
roses, roses that petal like words
written sweetly by Alice B., Alice belongs
to Gertrude's garden along with *Tender Buttons*,
tender planted kisses, not bachelor buttons
or Don Juan ramblers in our strong women's world,
our women's strong world, our world's
strong women cultivate strong gardens,
own our own gardens, tend our own
gardens, grow respect for Gertrude
Stein's garden where a weed would not grow,
a weed could not grow, a weed is afraid to root
on a rose is a rose is a rose.

MOVING TO THE COUNTRY

PETER NASH

THE PROPERTY CAME with a meadow and a hill that sloped down to the river, and a rutted dirt track that wound through pastures and pines. Tall bunch grass and wild oats fluttered in the silty soil. Golden poppies turned their faces to the sun while along the water, willows waved their fingers in the wind; a magical place, we both agreed, this green flat of grass and wild flowers enclosed in the bend of the river, cupped by low hills ascending to the sky.

In the middle of the meadow, stood the remains of an old house— all that was left of the Fitzsimmons homestead that had weathered half a century of neglect, winter rains, and dry summer winds. Across from the meadow stood a barn stuffed with ancient hay bales. Trunks of old books littered the floor. Rusted scythes, long saw blades and loops of barbed wire hung on the board walls

For years, my wife, Judy, and I had been coming to this rural area of Northern California looking for the perfect retirement spot while holding down the fort in our busy urban lives five hundred miles to the south. Even before walking through the dilapidated barn and the falling down homestead, Judy and I looked at each other, grinned, and decided to make an offer. Two days later our offer was accepted and we celebrated by gingerly lowering our pale bodies into one of the quiet pools along the river.

That spring we camped in the meadow and tried to make the house livable. Long ago others had camped in the living room and the beamed ceiling was black with greasy smoke. With the help of friends we sanded the ceiling and scraped soot and bird droppings from the windows. We painted the kitchen and rebuilt the porch railings. Pulling the battered linoleum off the floor, we found solid wide planks of barely damaged hardwood that we coated with linseed oil until it gleamed a shiny yellow brown. With the expertise of a local carpenter, a small bathroom with indoor plumbing was installed.

Each morning Judy and I would drink our coffee in the kitchen whose old-fashioned windowpanes of wavy glass made the tall bunch grass appear to ripple in the wind. While I could make a breakfast of cold cereal and fruit last until noon, Judy was always anxious to get going. "We can't just laze around while you stare at the meadow," she'd say and warn me of the fast approaching rainy season six months hence.

Judy and I had never worked together like this. Each of us chose a chore for the day and performed it at our own pace. I replaced the gutters while Judy meticulously painted the inside of our little house a warm white with a pale yellow trim. There were boxes to unpack, pictures to hang, junk to be trucked to the dump. She and I became closer. The hours and days flew by. Spring became summer, the meadow changed to light green, then gold and finally the typical California bleached out brown. By September, our house was complete. Neither elegant nor charming, it was at least habitable, and we could work on it for the next 10 years for its beauty to emerge.

I turned my attention to the small barn behind a grove of bay laurels. I swept out decomposing bales of hay filled with coffin-shaped mouse droppings and thousands of shreds of gnawed paper. I filled most of the ground floor with neatly stacked firewood. While the hay burned, I would sit in front of the barn with my binoculars and soar high above the valley with the vultures black against the blue sky. I flew with the ravens into the dark firs.

Wading through thigh-high oats one afternoon, I came home in rollicking spirits. The barn was as clean as it would ever be. In equally high spirits, Judy announced that she had arranged with a neighboring rancher to mow the meadow and rototill the front yard. It was time to prepare her garden before the winter drove us inside.

I knew that Judy was going to put in a garden. I had lived with her for 30 years in a house littered with gardening magazines on every table. I had helped carry bags of manure, disposed of plastic containers holding her young starts, sympathized with her over plants lost to gophers and the ubiquitous snail. Each spring I had cheerfully paid our local nursery bills as Judy gamely tried to establish one plant after another in the small shady space that surrounded our house.

❋

It had been my idea to move. Judy loved living in the friendly university town where she had worked for three decades as a nurse practitioner. Patients and acquaintances would hail her in the supermarket and the dry cleaners. She was as familiar with each store and road sign as her own kitchen that we had just remodeled. She loved her new granite counters against the board-and-batten walls combining a feeling of antiquity with modern convenience. For Judy, our home was like a beloved and eccentric parent–a 100-year-old farmhouse with randomly tacked-on rooms, each with its own characteristic creaky floor. She loved the wainscoting, the ancient crown molding, and the memories of kids raised, parties given, holiday excitement. Now that the kids were gone we were like two seeds rattling around in a huge and costly gourd.

Judy's biggest trial had been our shady yard the size of a postage-stamp. Growing anything in that garden except ferns, fuschias, and rhododendrons was not easy. But Judy never stopped trying. Even as we grew older and her energy flagged, Judy was not ready to give up. Eventually the house would become too much to maintain but she was not ready to admit that.

But I, I was going to retire shortly and wanted to move full steam ahead. I was ready to live in the country for I had never given up my dream of "going back to the land." I was ready for an adventure while we were still healthy and I hadn't lost my youthful spirit. "Perhaps our last great adventure," I would mutter darkly, "before I spend my final days in the nursing home."

Continuing the familiar discussion on a more positive note, I would add, "Here's your chance to fulfill your dream of the ultimate garden." Then, with the zeal of a used car salesman, I would rhapsodize about the virtues of living in the country with a garden as wide and sunny as the sky, the unpolluted soil so rich that anything would grow. My trump card was always the same: the only way we could afford to retire was to sell our house and buy country property.

Judy is eminently practical. We moved, though she shed many tears.

And yet, now that I had uprooted my wife from her familiar surroundings, though I had promised her a garden as wide and sunny as the sky, I discovered that I was reluctant to interfere with the beautiful meadow surrounding us. It seemed a sacrilege to mow and rototill it, and then to plant it with exotic, non-native shrubs. I loved this meadow just as it was. The magenta foxglove nodded to me on their spiky stalks. The coyote bush beckoned with its tough leaves and white flowers like bright birthday candles. There was no need to maintain the bay trees, the young Douglas firs, the wild blackberries with their creeping vines, the rustling grasses. All grew naturally and without any effort of mine. Deer bounded across the meadow making perfect arches, foxes dove into the underbrush, black vultures like ancient judges crowded the topmost branches of lightning-blasted oaks. And so while Judy ruffled through gardening magazines I read about the original hunting and gathering inhabitants of this small Northern California valley. Like Adam and Eve, they had lived off the land without planting or tilling. I began to feel that if humans could just leave the land alone, not touch it or improve it or garden it, the land would slowly revert to its natural form. Given enough time the land would reassert itself. Roads would crumble, telephone lines would topple, houses would collapse of their own weight. The salmon would return, huge elk would browse in the ravines, lightning fires would periodically burn the underbrush into a park-like setting. I imagined wolves slowly making their way down from the Arctic while tall prairie grass took over the coastal meadows.

How Judy and I fit into my fantasy of wild prehistoric America was unclear. All that I knew was that I wanted to preserve the land as it was. I wanted to watch it grow into itself. I did not want to make it into a garden, a vineyard, or a feedlot for cattle.

But of course that was impossible. Judy is no more capable of observing an unplanted patch of land without planning to improve it then I am of assembling a locomotive from scratch. "Get rid of all this poison oak," she once said waving her arms toward the far reaches of the valley. She wanted me to mow the entire prairie, uproot the sticker-y milk thistle with its lime green cups, line the slim deer trails with river rock and plant fruit trees in every conceivable space. Judy's picture of paradise is a weed-free intensely cultivated garden while I can think of nothing more lovely then watching the slow encroachment of a natural forest onto a wild meadow.

96

We struck a compromise. Outside the fence I was king. I decreed no new roads, no junked vehicles, no mowing, digging or planting. Inside the deer-proof fence that enclosed about three acres, Judy ruled supreme. "Anything you want," I told her. We erected a potting shed, laid out compost heaps and raised beds that I built from discarded lumber, and which she continues to extravagantly praise even as they pull apart at the corners.

Judy put the garden in by herself. Double digging, she piled the weeds to the side of the turned field in rank tangles. She flung dark shovel-fulls of peat moss and fertilizer onto the raw ground and eased dozens of roses blooming in their gallon cans into the chocolate earth. She planted the potted salvia, the wrinkled seeds of nasturtiums, the tender starts of carrots and Early Girl tomatoes. She planted three kinds of summer squash, hard kernels of sweet corn, chunky eyes of potatoes and though it was the wrong time of the year, she buried the iris bulbs in deep. She was like an iridescent hummingbird in a hot haze of motion.

I marveled at the blur of her tan, competent hands patting the soil, her oiled joints, the short solid build she inherited from her father who raised his family on 20 acres of grapes in the Central Valley.

She is the last link in a long line of farmers that stretches back to Armenia. She loves the feel of dirt between her palms, the shovel against her boot, the pull of the hose against her hip, the heft of buckets dragging her shoulders. Sometimes I see her crouching close to the earth inhaling the rough viney smell of green tomatoes.

Now that the house is finished, I read a lot and write, indulging my dream of becoming a published poet. I stack wood, and mow the lawn on a tractor mower. I often sit in my canvas director's chair and watch Judy as she squats before some green sprig, her lips moving. But mostly, I find myself meandering along the riverbank or sitting with my back against a Douglas fir. I gather wild blackberries and enter the secret rooms of willow groves where sparrows flit from branch to branch. Some days I can be found lying in the meadow following the clouds like white galleons as they sail over the green horizons. Once Judy discovered me with my ear to the ground listening for the myriad of beating hearts beneath the grass.

If it were up to me there would be no garden. But I'd miss the bouquets of lavender on our dining room table. I'd miss the candy-striped zinnias, the kale, the cabbage, the curved cucumbers, the purple onions. And I'd miss the bustle of Judy's sturdy form, the sheen of light on her damp face and the way she offers me an armful of perfumed stock and how she enters the house at dusk, sweating, flushed, smudged, breathing quickly as after sex, and wanting only to wash her hands and drink a glass of spring water before starting dinner.

97

And so I sit on the porch, reading, slyly watching my wife. And I realize that I could not bear to see the coyote bush and milk thistle take over. I pick up my book again, and think of fresh salad tonight, the vase of cut flowers, sweet corn.

98

POLITICS AND CANNED TOMATOES

NANCY WERKING POLING

DURING THE SUMMER of 1973—while I canned 50 quarts of tomatoes, 50 quarts of tomato juice, 20 pints of tomato sauce, and 12 pints of catsup—Men in Power were asking, "What did Nixon know and when did he know it?" Toiling in my narrow kitchen, with its five feet of counter space, Youngstown metal sink, and antediluvian four-burner electric stove, I fervently followed the Senate Watergate Hearings on a 15-inch black-and-white TV. I wanted answers, too.

Frequently I'd interrupt the flow of work to wipe my sweating forehead with the tail of my sleeveless blouse. Operating all at once, the four stove burners rivaled a Bessemer in emitting BTUs. Blue and white speckled enamel canners occupied two burners; on another, a large tea kettle maintained a low whistle. On the front left burner, the one nearest the sink, a pan of water boiled.

As Tom Daschel posed questions to men who'd sworn to tell the truth, the whole truth, and nothing but the truth, I prepared tomatoes for easy peeling by briefly immersing them in the pan of boiling water. Nixon was in hot water, too, and everyone knew him to be a sweating man, even when he sat in the air-conditioned Oval Office signing his now besmirched name. Had he been in my kitchen, the heat would have convinced him he was already in hell.

While H.R. Haldeman scalded the truth, I stuffed whole tomatoes into quart Mason jars, which I filled to the top with boiling water from the tea kettle. From a saucepan resting on the sink drain, I lifted sterilized lids, placed them on the jars with tongs, then screwed on the metal rings. The whole country was getting screwed.

After placing seven filled jars in the wire racks of both canners, I gently lowered the heavy racks into the boiling water bath. Pausing to rest a moment while the stove and canners carried out their responsibilities, I sat at the kitchen table staring at the TV, engrossed in Daniel Inouye's line of questioning.

The simple life—that was the path my husband, Jim, and I had chosen. Self-sufficiency. A quarter of an acre in tomatoes, corn, peas, green beans, and other vegetables, enough filled glass jars on basement shelves and cardboard boxes in our twenty-cubic-foot freezer to feed us until the next harvest. Quite an accomplishment for a young woman who'd grown up in the city and a young man whose previous gardening experience had been limited to picking green beans for his mother to cook for dinner or reluctantly weeding alongside his father.

Twenty holes filled with water, 20 tomato plants, their stems wrapped in strips of paper grocery bags to protect them from boring insects. In 1973 our young bodies were agile. For hours we could bend over a hoe, work on our knees, gently place the tomato plants in the holes, pack the muddy soil around them.

"Now I'm just a country lawyer," Sam Erwin said, obviously shrewd in spite of his self-deprecating performance. A country lawyer butting heads with urbane fellows acting as if they were above the law. Stepping away from the stove to cool off, sweeping a strand of wet hair from my face, I pictured Erwin as a young man, laboring in a garden not unlike ours. Dirt caked our hands, got underneath our fingernails. Had Erwin's hands once looked the same way? Surely those of Haldeman and Ehrlichman were well-manicured.

Contrary to what we'd assumed, maintaining a successful garden required much more than planting and hoeing. We relied on neighbors for how-to advice. We read Rodale publications, subscribed to organic gardening magazines, some of which suggested that gardeners keep records of what they planted and when. Yes, the simple life was far more complicated than we'd anticipated.

Life was turning out to be complicated for John Dean, as well, who testified for seven hours one day. But he'd kept records, could tell the senators what Nixon and Haldeman and Ehrlichman had said in his presence. Pulling the weeds of deception out by the roots, he was.

My glasses steamed as I lifted the racks out of the canners. One by one I carried the hot jars to the counter, lining them up on layers of dish towels, then beginning the process all over again: dipping whole tomatoes into boiling water, stuffing clean jars, filling the jars to their tops with boiling water, putting on lids, lowering them into the water bath.

Our garden was a political statement, something young people of the 1960s needed to do to declare our disdain for the Establishment. We refused to buy into the capitalist dream, shunning the symbols of affluence and power. Everything on my little TV set supported that decision. The government was corrupt, and the Watergate hearings were proving it.

Still, I was shocked, when on a July day, while I was adding spices to a batch of catsup, Alexander Butterfield testified that Nixon recorded conversations and phone calls. To make sure I didn't miss anything, I walked away from the pan to stand next to the TV. By the time I returned to the stove the catsup was sticking to the bottom of the pan, scorched, ruined.

As jars on my kitchen counter cooled, the lids would one-by-one ping, evidence that the jars were sealed. When they were cool, I carried them, two at a time, down the basement steps, back into a small dark room lined with shelves. Symbols of Jim's labor and my own, they stood at attention, row upon row of them.

When I dropped in bed each night exhausted, in those brief moments before I fell asleep, I considered the sleepless nights many in Washington were experiencing, innocent and guilty alike: Senators Howard Baker and Lowell Weiker worrying about how the Republican Party would ever recover; Charles Colson and G. Gordan Liddy becoming aware that they might spend years in prison; Butterfield and Dean, no doubt fretting about betraying those they'd worked for. Then of course, Nixon himself. He couldn't be sleeping well.

Why was I so obsessed with watching the Watergate Hearings? In many ways they were like a soap opera, where any minute the plot can take an unexpected turn. At times I imagined background music changing tempo, becoming more somber as the drama built. Yet, I, like many other Americans, sensed that history was being made, that bringing down a president was no light matter, that the country would never be the same.

There was probably a more personal reason, as well. In spite of our goal of self-reliance, I recognized that we could never be separate. Just as we had vowed to stay married for better or for worse, we were a part of this country for better or for worse. As much as we were trying to isolate ourselves from capitalist society, we were tied to its fate.

102

THE MAN THAT GREW IN MY GARDEN

LAURIE POLLOCK

FOR YEARS I dreamed of spending a week at the house in May, putting things right in the garden. In the Hudson Valley, where my family spends our weekends, spring comes late. It isn't until Mothers' Day that the lilacs start blooming and the ground becomes warm and ready. In the garden, suddenly everything seems possible.

When I finally quit my job, I realized I could take a week to garden if I wanted to–and then, even better, Ian decided he wanted to come with me. My son Ian didn't go to college along with the rest of his friends. He was sick of being a student. He wanted to "try the actor-waiter thing." But after his friends left town for their various colleges in the fall, he was a little lonely. He started coming up to the house on weekends and began dreaming, too. Not the same dream as mine, but a related dream—a vegetable patch of his own, big enough for his own crops. While I wanted to bring some order to the life I had, he wanted to build a new garden from scratch, create his own turf.

103

Ian had spent eight long summers in Vermont at a camp that was an organic farm. He knew exactly what he wanted. He led me down to a piece of deeply sodded meadow at the bottom of the wall holding up my garden, and said, "This is the place," with all the solemnity of Brigham Young at Salt Lake. He would have to dig it up, fence it in, net it over against the birds and deer, enrich the soil and plant it.

There was one tiny further complication. His plot included the area where my composter was—a perfect spot because it was close to the house, but hidden. So I had a new project added to my list: to find another place for the composter. Ian helped me scout a good location near the kitchen, up a little bank behind some lilacs. Then he pulled on his boots and went off with a garden fork, while I dug a new space for the composter to sit securely, and built two steps up, held in place by logs that were too long for the fireplace. I pounded in huge railroad spikes at either end of the logs to keep them secure and filled in the spaces with dirt. Then I moved the composter, and planted grass seed on the new earth steps. First job done!

I went to get a glass of water and wash my hands. How satisfying it was to look out my kitchen window and see the seeded steps, held by logs, leading up behind the lilacs. And now I could start on the kitchen-door herb garden I'd always wanted.

I could hear Ian forking his patch at the bottom of the hill. The old pasture soil, too stony to plow, was full of egg-sized rocks. He filled bucket after bucket with them. I could hear them scrape, then thud, as he dumped them out in the woods. On my way into the kitchen to get string, I took a long detour down the hill to see.

Shirtless in the sun, dark curls escaping from his Red Sox cap, he was putting his back into his task. He turned and threw a stone that looked like a baked potato into the bucket. He has the physical grace to be an actor, I thought. Does he have the looks? He turned and smiled at me. Oh, yes he does.

"I've forked this whole space four times," he said. "They sneak up on me when my back is turned." He drove his fork into the soft earth and turned up three or four new stones. "See?" He took off his cap and wiped his face with the back of his arm.

I came back with two icy glasses of water and we rested awhile, sitting on the warm earth and tossing stones into the bucket. Definitely no carrots this year, we decided—not with the soil this rocky. Why do new rocks poke their cold noses up above the earth every day? Every time I turn over my garden, it's full of stones. I pull them out, year after year, work in compost and manure – and the next year it's the same story. Something about frost heaves, I've been told. But then why don't they ever heave downward?

"Do you think they migrate toward the warmth of the sun?" I suggested.

"Yeah, like seeds sprouting. Maybe they're the seeds of something." Suddenly Ian laughed out loud. "Stone walls! That's why all the old stone walls in the woods are falling down. They've gone to seed."

He got up to empty the bucket, and started forking over the area again. His fork stuck on something deep in the soil. Something big. He put his weight into it but couldn't move it. He got the fork under the big rock and tried again to shift it. *Snap!*

Rock 1, Ian 0.

Ian threw down the gap-toothed fork and went to get a spade out of the shed. I returned to my herb garden. But after a while, tired and sunburned, I walked back down the hill to watch his progress. He had excavated the dirt all around the rock. It was as big as a Thanksgiving turkey. Working the shovel around it, he pried it loose, then heaved it up onto the surface. The conqueror carried his vanquished enemy to the old stone wall and dropped it. He pulled a stalk of grass and put it between his teeth. The sun was going golden. The earth smelled rich and fresh. It was a good day's work.

Ian picked up his T-shirt from the ground and waved it at the mosquitoes beginning to encircle us. "Time for a beer, don't you think, Mom?"

I was a little shocked. We'd never given him a drink, and he knew perfectly well that we wouldn't until he was 21. But I was impressed at how hard he'd worked all day, on a job that turned out much harder than he'd expected. And he gave me that smile. Oh, that smile. I made a face like I was thinking it over.

"Yeah, OK," I said.

It was still cool enough in the evening for a fire. We called my husband, Michael, at the apartment and told him our various triumphs. We scratched our mosquito bites. We ate chicken and salad. We played Scrabble on the rug, and I suspect he let me win. At 9:30, when I got in bed with my gardening encyclopedia, I was utterly happy.

The next day, we got up with the sun. My goal was to move some 20-year-old peonies out of my perennial garden. Around their roots I found thousands of little bulbs that were too deep to bloom and replanted them closer to the surface.

Ian was hard at work. His vegetable patch was going to have to be securely deer-proof, and he had a plan.

"Do you want some help?"

"No."

"Have you made a sketch?"

"No. Why should I?"

"Because that's the right way. You make a scale drawing, and measure, and figure everything out beforehand. That's how you know what you have to do."

"That's how *you* know what you have to do, Mom. I know what I'm going to do."

"Okay," I said, swallowing what I was thinking.

He disappeared into the woods with an axe over his shoulder, swinging his boots into long strides. I heard thwack-thwack, and the sh-sh-shh of branches swaying. All the time I was dividing my peonies, I heard thwack-thwack. Thwack-thwack-thwack. I had replanted eight of them in new holes along the drive, when Ian reappeared carrying a couple of long skinny maple saplings. Chewing on a piece of grass, he stood up one of the saplings at the corner of his patch, squinted at it for a long minute, then sawed it off. When he tried it again, I saw what he was getting at – an elegant plan for natural arches over the garden like springy ribs, so he could cover the whole with deer netting. It was going to be beautiful. Only he had sawed off the maple too short. He had to go cut another. "Mom, do we have a sharpening stone?" he sighed. That day he learned two of life's greatest lessons: 1. Sharpen your axe before you begin. 2. Measure twice, cut once. And I was glad I had let him learn them by himself.

As the sun went down, we lit the barbecue. Over steaks and baked potatoes, I showed him how to sketch his plan out to scale, and measure both in the plan and on the ground. He made a pattern. I made suggestions. The next morning, he paced it out. He stretched string along the ground and measured. He made notes and diagrams, and a list of the things he'd need: 4x4's for the corner posts, wire fencing and the right kind of nails, deer netting, and a hook and eye for the gate.

The next stop was the lumberyard.

We pulled up and looked at the flannel-shirted guys expertly backing up their pickups, the big-armed guys slinging sacks of concrete and bundles of boards, the guys with John Deere caps spitting in the sawdust. Ripsaws whined.

"I'll let you out. Got your list?"

He exhaled. "Yep."

He swung out of the Volvo. I parked and went to look at drawer pulls and cabinet knobs, because there are places you can go with your mother, but the lumberyard is not one of them. When he came strolling back with his custom-cut boards over his shoulder, his Red Sox cap at a rakish angle, he was whistling. He seemed a little taller, and the straggly stubble he'd been growing looked a little beardier. His dark eyes sparkled. I was at work when Ian took his first baby steps, but I got to witness the first steps of a young man who knows his way around a lumberyard. Thank God he hadn't got his driver's license yet! If he'd just come home in the car, I would have missed that milestone.

We stopped to buy manure, peat moss, seeds and seedlings, and to replace the garden fork. I bought rosemary, marjoram, Greek oregano, two kinds of sage, two kinds of thyme, mint and chives. We discussed the merits of various kinds of tomatoes, and chose five varieties—Amish Plum for cooking, Brandywine for slicing, Sungold Cherries and Yellow Pears for snacking and salads, and Mortgage Lifter beefsteaks, because who could resist the story of tomatoes that grew so huge, the guy who bred them was able to pay off his house?

Before we knocked off for the night, Ian came up to the perennial garden where I was tugging at the deep roots of an ancient yucca that was there when we moved in and had been irking me every summer for 20 years. When Ian was little, he called it the "yucky plant."

"Here, I'll do that," he said. He struck the new fork deep into the yucca's heart and lifted it like the head of Medusa, dripping with soil. He carried it to the brush pile.

"Can you help me with my netting, Mom?"

"Of course," I said. "I'm done for today, and I haven't had a look."

Carved into the meadow was a beautiful garden: deeply dug, with a sturdy fence, three slim maple arches over the top, and a tidy gate with a maple-branch X on it. We stretched the netting over the top and secured it along the fence-top. Everything was ready for planting.

After waffles the next morning, he showed me how to build a teepee of poles for beans, where I'd always let them straggle along the fence. He planted Hubbard and butternut squash in hills around the bottom of the teepee, the way the Indians traditionally planted the Three Sisters: beans, squash and corn. He planted peppers, and he taught me that the sweet must go upwind from the hot, because if they cross-pollinate, they'll all be hot. The shoe was on the other foot.

It's wonderful to teach things to your kids. It's wonderful to watch them figure out how to do things for themselves. If you're lucky, at some point your child will teach you something you don't know anything about. But when your child can teach you more than you knew, can surpass your knowledge in your own field, that's the sweetest of all.

108

BERRIES ON MY TONGUE

MICHELE HEATHER POLLOCK

THE EARTH AT the surface is warm from the August sun, but grows cooler and wetter as I bury my fingers like roots, wiggle them like worms until the dirt crumbles. I am bored with this garden, so I am playing in the dirt like a child. I am bored, so I am procrastinating. I look around my respectable square of earth–nobly cleared of grass and weeds in the spring; dutifully protected from rabbits by an effective, if unsightly, length of chicken wire; symmetrically planted in parallel rows of useful vegetables. Considering my enthusiasm at the start of the season, I am surprised now, kneeling in the warm August dirt, to realize that this list continues with: hesitantly weeded too infrequently; begrudgingly watered almost daily; harvested with much less gratification than my May mind could have imagined.

109

The peppers are useful for kabobs, yes, and the tomatoes for sandwiches and salsa and sauces. My abundance of radishes and carrots are either bursting from the ground waiting to be pulled, sitting on the counter waiting to be washed, or packaged in the fridge waiting for the salads I never seem to make. I don't have a taste for them. But I wanted to be a gardener! Last winter I spent hours turning the glossy pages of magazines, memorizing Martha's satisfaction at culling out abundance from the raw materials of the earth, imagining my own inner glow as I chopped and sautéed my hard-won miracles of growth. At this moment, as I ignore for a few minutes longer the drooping pepper plants' leaves and the cilantro gone to seed, I enjoy only feeling dirt in my hands. I am tempted to leave all of this to fight its own battle with the weeds, to fend for itself until the next rain. After all, I don't even *like* tomatoes.

This garden is like my work life. Organized. Productive. Useful. My career is a respectable one, well-planned, with my time and energy all neatly fenced in and allocated, my tasks aligned in parallel rows, goals growing like peppers and tomatoes, fertilized by my education, watered by my dedication. I spent years in college planting the seeds of this garden, yearning for the ultimate satisfaction that harvesting success would bring.

Everything I produce is useful, nutritious, in theory good for me. I have all the tools to do it well, and the potential harvest is large. So why do I resent the time spent within this garden fence? Why do I daily weed and water, maintain the plot, when I don't even like what I produce?

I brush the dirt from my hands, straddle the fence and head for the raspberry patch. I literally "discovered" it this summer—a huge patch, years beyond overgrowth into chaos, at the back of the property. But the unruly plants are producing. New berries are constantly emerging, hard and green, from the bases of white flowers. I see fully ripened berries, offered up to the sky on canes extending like arms. Deep red, juicy berries that the birds adore. Sweet luxury food that nature has produced for years without not only my help, but without even my knowledge. No fence will work here; the predators have wings.

A few berries are within reach, but the majority I can see are in the center of the patch. The first time I saw the berries, ignorant and craving their tart redness, I stepped eagerly into the patch. Soon enough, scratched and bleeding, I discovered the thorns. The berries were sweet, but came at a price. I learned to prepare myself, cover my arms and legs even in the summer sun. Or I learned to take a deep breath and endure the prickly pain for a mouthful of fruit. Today I crave the raspberries, so I pull on a long-sleeved shirt, even in the heat of this August afternoon, and fight my way through the thorns guarding the swelling fruit. I pick a few ripe berries and eat them right here, smashing them between my tongue and the roof of my mouth, enjoying the juices. Here I don't have to weed, to water, to cajole and primp, fertilize and pinch back. The earth produces this fruit despite herself, manages an abundance of luxury, a dessert on tenacious branches that can win their own battles with weeds.

What I have to do is find the berries, be patient enough to let them ripen. Then I have choices. I can consume them right here among the brambles, raw and unwashed and tart, for the sheer pleasure of the berries. Or I can gather them, take them inside, and wash them. I can put them on ice cream, make them into jam. I can make tarts or pie. Or raspberry iced tea. I can let the raspberry patch survive and produce on its own and take what it gives me, while I spend my energy in my fenced garden. Or I can check out a book from the library and learn how to improve and refine this abundance of nature. I can learn which canes to cut back in the fall, how to thin the weaker branches so the stronger ones don't have to struggle for sunlight. I can be a gardener, but one of a different kind.

The patch of berries is like my artistic life. The potential is there and the words and images want to come, even if I don't tend the patch.

110

I've discovered poetry in myself, and it grows and produces despite itself. I've also discovered the thorns that make it difficult to enjoy the fruit: the inner critic, lack of time, fear. I can take the few ripe words available to me at the edge, if I am content with them, and consume them on the spot, juices of their meaning running down my chin, an easy treat that I keep all to myself. Or I can make more of it, encouraging their growth, thinning out the weakness so the strengths can see the sun. I can create for myself the long sleeves I need to face the thorns, to reach the fruit in the middle. I can pair words with time and experience, serve them up with form and substance. I can become poet and artist, gardener of raspberries. Or I can keep tending to my fenced-in garden, learn to like tomatoes while the birds eat the berries or, over-ripe, they fall uneaten to the ground.

The berries are here, whether I take advantage of them or not, but I will have to spend time outside my fenced-in area to find them. I will. I will eat some on the spot. I will gather more for later. I will share some with the birds. There are enough for all. And one of these springs, with the taste of last year's berries on my tongue, I might not even plant tomatoes at all.

AUSTRIAN PINE IN APRIL

Doris J. Popovich

Handsome gray-brown bark expands,
Inhaling our joy about the changing season.
Wood veins and timber nerves
Deliver the sun's invitation

To sleepy wistful roots
Who secretly pine for a few more days;
April for *Pinus nigra*
A month of Monday mornings.

112

Uncombed branches wake up
Slowly from their half-sleep.
Some remember to reach up
Right away,

While others
More Taurian by nature
Remain low, stout and spreading;
More persistent in their prickle.

Seduced by warm days in May,
Soaring trees surrender, soften.
Spring needles deepen
To a lustrous dark green.

Feather-tip new life clusters,
Tawny-yellow and soft,
Whisper wisdom about
Resilience, fortitude and grace.

THE GARDENER

MICHAEL RATTEE

She plants and it rains
for the lack of a plan
it seems magical
but it is only
the chance of weather
predicted by arthritis
and old scars
a way to blame the past
and praise the future
but for now she's happy
the desert soil growing
dark with dampness
assures her that things
are as they should be
she stands in the rain
rejoicing her good luck
feeling like a seed herself
about to split open
and accept the elements
she can almost feel
the world spinning
towards another year
and for the moment
even that feels good
and with a single shouted word
she jumps into the first puddle
the entire garden laughing with her

BOUGAINVILLEA

KATHRYN RIDALL

Queen of our garden,
your lush south-of-the-border beauty
presides over the feathered wands
of lavender, the crisp-petaled daisies
with their girl-next-door innocence,
over even the rhododendron
with their bursting crimson bells.

I wonder: how do you bear the sideways
glances of your blossomed sisters, the slight
drooping of their petals when you display
your cape of fuchsia stars?

Bougainvillea, shining diva of the garden,
you sing your flaming arias with no apology.
You teach me—never hold back.

PERSEPHONE

JESSICA BANE ROBERT

Under the rock wall bend, earthworms start
to slow inside their shrinking skins. Vines snake
toward the canopy, unable to outslither yellowing.
Under the wind-leaf cacophony, on the toe-bones
of an oak with an ear to its gray-green chest, listen.
The tree gurgles its lullaby sky to earth, earth
to sky—in every inch a universe is humming.

Spring, a crocus ghost hung on the cellar door;
the Earth contracts quelling her mysteries
like whimpering children folded into her breast.
Stand long and still to hear the season going
heavily down, into beautiful, familiar darkness.

WHITE GARDEN

Sylvia Forges-Ryan

Just say that once she loved
This garden in all its casts
Of white. The choreography
Of blooms rising up one row
At a time, the shortest ones
First, ascending to the back
In vulnerable order.

Say that it made her glad
To see the crocus tips nudge
Through the final smear of snow.
And the long stemmed tulips,
Making their appearance so soon
After, turning always for the light,
Stirred her heart toward song.

Say that she took the measure
Of its rhythms, that she was awed
By the delicate condescension
In all that bending and unfolding.

They say something in her also
Danced, when, at the grand finale,
The daylilies would rise
Unfailingly elegant, unfailingly brief
Above extravagant fountains of green.

LOVE IN ROSES

LYNN VEACH SADLER

[After Roses in the Lady Norwood Rose Garden, Wellington, New Zealand]

He'd been the *Happy Wanderer*.
He needed his *First Love, Love Story*.
They introduced him to
Wellington's most eligible:
Candella, Soraya, Carina, Youki San,
Kaikoura, Jadis . . . .
Did he want a *Lolita*?
An *Amazon*? A she *Ice White*?
A *Tzigane*?

But it was *Sheila's Perfume*
that caught him.
"*Holy Toledo!*" all said.
"Not *Dainty Dinah*, not *Dame Cath!*"
Well, Sheila was *Pristine*—
and a *Stargazer, Sparkler.*
Could sing like *Maria Callas*,
write like *Katherine Mansfield*,
act like *Ingrid Bergman*.

For his wedding gift, he gave Sheila
a *Claude Monet* and one *Old Master*.
When she caught blight and died,
he planted the Lady Kerryman Rose Garden
in her honor, sits there every afternoon
in *Sunblaze* to think of her.
His favorite rose?
The *Remember Me*.

THE COMPOST BIN

ELLEN SEUSY

All winter, and in all seasons,
I feed this dirt from my own kitchen,
taking the long walk into a deep yard.

Out of the yellow light of the house,
stepping down from the din of appliances,
out of rooms stuffy with television,

I sink into a pool of light on the snow
and pause to balance two bowls
heavy with limp celery and red cabbage.

At the edge of the light, I look down,
then step into Ohio's dark night,
into what used to be forest.

The yard is quiet. This cold walk through the dark
takes me far. Who knows what will bloom
from what I bring? At the wooden bin

I tip the bowls onto the snowed-over compost.
Chemistry is going on in there
that I don't understand; pink peonies

could come from this decay. Sometimes
I wish not to go back, but to stay out
by the soft-armed hemlocks,

out here by the compost bin,
this hearth way in the back of the yard,
and deep inside, the fire that no one lit.

TAKING THAT BITE BEFORE LEAVING

SUSAN BALLER-SHEPARD

I can't remember how it started. As we strolled out of
the trees and onto the savannah, did I pick it carelessly
as we walked hand in hand, then with my lips on yours and
yours groping for mine, with that hunger did I take the bite
right there in front of God and everybody?

Or had I planned to take what was not mine?
It's been long enough that my calculations
are lost to me, except for this: that the deed is done.

It was cold and hard, tart, dripping down my arm, such
a fine contrast to your warm mouth on mine, right after
that bite, you eating it with me, but *my* tooth marks on the skin.

I pack and leave after that, the place lost its thrill. No more
the sweet fruit of life's tree, no longer crisp delights from
the tree of the wise, I have one child after another who can't
get along but still sometimes
I dream

...we are back, we have not gone too far. We are still
pristine. Life is easy. We have all we need.
We still have His scent and luminescence.

I awake
with a start, and a weep, reach out for your
skin as I knew it then, uncovered, without all
these accouterments, minus all these layers.

IN the RAIN FOREST with a NEWLY SINGLE FRIEND

JEAN SHEPARD

It was like walking
through a fig,
seeds and strings
of sweetness everywhere.
We were breathing inside
a honey jar, and we saw
wal- to-wall green;
I'd have to call it
ruby green. Rain forest?
More a condensed-milk
forest. I remember
wondering where the
crickets were as silence
cracked around my ears,
and I thought surely my blood was
on the wrong side of my body.
When we came to the end,
we stepped out of the milky way
into the sweetness of space.
Then as I imagined your new life
with its glut of flesh,
my gills opened red to the sky.

120

GARDEN PESTS

GRAZINA SMITH

"OH, NO! I can't believe this!" I moaned and ran my nail along the rose bud. A thick smear of green, sticky aphids coated my thumb. I wiped them on my shirtsleeve and saw that all my Sonia rosebuds were bumpy with aphids. They had appeared overnight and the garden show was just a week away.

"I'd do anything to get rid of them," I whispered.

"And what would you be willing to do?" A voice behind me asked.

I jumped, turned around and saw a short, roly-poly man standing in my yard. He grinned and his dark mischievous eyes reflected his mirth. He wore a brown, three-piece suit that was much too tight and warm for the weather. A small cheroot hung from his teeth. The cheap cigar's blue smoke encircled his head like a thundercloud. His nose twitched jiggling his thin mustache.

"How did you get in to my back yard?" I demanded.

"Through the gate," he shrugged, "but does it matter? Do you want to get rid of the aphids and win the garden show?"

"Of course I do but what can you do about it?"

He stepped past me, inhaled deeply on his cheroot and blew the inky smoke at my rose buds.

"Stop! You'll kill them!"

I pushed him away, coughing and fanning my hand to clear the smoke. A plump clean rosebud appeared. Light purple petals peeked from the calyx and the bud was greener, healthier, than it had been a minute ago.

"What did you do?" I turned and faced him. "Who are you?"

"I'm Velnukas, and like Cher, I go by just one name," he said. "If you really want to win first place in the flower show, I can make it happen."

"Well, Mr. Val-new-cuss, (I pronounced his name carefully), how can you make it happen?" I paused. "And what's it going to cost me?"

"Nothing if you don't win...but think what it'll mean if you can beat Janet."

Janet! My jaw clenched at the mention of her name. How did he know about Janet? She's been my nemesis since the first day of kindergarten. Janet came in the room with bouncy blonde curls and a big smile on her face. She wore fancy dresses, starched white pinafores and patent leather shoes. Janet simpered and smiled her way into teachers' hearts. I had tight, wiry orange hair that curled into a Harpo Marx tangle. My mother thought Buster Brown lace-ups and dark, plaid shirtwaists were the school uniform. When called on to recite, I stuttered and turned red. For years, my teachers told me to take a deep breath and slow down. They couldn't understand a word I said.

In high school, Janet won most of the academic honors, was head cheerleader, got the lead in the school play and was valedictorian. Of course, she dated the captain of the football team. I was always trailing behind–to be honest, not even in the same league. My grades were never great. I wasn't athletic. I painted scenery for the play and went to the prom with the school nerd and even he cast cow-eyes at Janet as we stumbled around the dance floor.

You'd think I'd get over high school competition–and I would have, if it hadn't followed me through life. Janet got the jobs I wanted, the man I lusted after and that place in our community where "dear, good Janet" could do no wrong. I couldn't even complain about her to anyone without sounding petty and vindictive. I always greeted her with a tight, constipated smile. My only way to compete with her was the garden show and I always lost, never even making it into the top ten! My arrangements were "too minimalist," or "too crowded," or "too asymmetric"; I guess that's a polite way of saying "weird." Sometimes my flowers drooped before the judges even got to the table. Janet didn't always win first place but she always won a ribbon for something. I swear, they'd give her one just for showing up. The whole garden show fiasco was a metaphor for my life.

"Yes, Janet," I sighed. "I saw her yesterday at the beauty shop. How do you know about her?"

"Well," he said in a slow dreamy voice, "wouldn't it be wonderful to finally beat her?"

"You bet!" I snapped. That slipped out before I could stop myself. Yesterday, she waved at me as she left the beauty shop. "I'll see you next week at the garden show," she purred. I swear that woman loves to rub it in.

Of course, her blonde hair had turned lustrous silver and she wears it in a sleek pageboy. She's aged well and could model for those hormone replacement ads where women look as if they're photographed through a filter. My hair stayed wiry and unmanageable and now, chopped short, it looks like a poodle's gray rump. And wrinkles? There probably isn't enough Botox in the whole town to smooth my face, one of the bonuses of working in the garden. Not that I care about the wrinkles, but it would be nice to show Janet, just once, that I can do something right. I looked at that short, fat man.

"How do you know about Janet and me?" I asked him again.

"Oh, I know many things about you and, especially, how badly you want to win the garden show."

"Who are you? A stalker or something?" He was making me nervous and I started edging toward the kitchen door. *Maybe I should call the police.*

"Wait...well, I don't know how to put this...how can I explain who I am?" he sighed. "You know the movie, *It's a Wonderful Life?*" I nodded.

"Well," he sighed again and rolled his eyes. "Angels aren't the only ones who have to work to win their wings..." I stared at him, not comprehending what he said.

"You know, the other side has to work, too." It slowly dawned on me.

"You think you're the devil?" I looked around for a quick escape.

"I don't *THINK* I'm the devil..." he snapped.

Great, I was alone in my back yard with a nut who believed he was the devil. I was afraid to turn away from him and began to slowly creep backward toward the door.

"Wait! Wait! What can I do to show you?" He madly waved his cheroot in the air and a maelstrom of sparks scattered around us.

"Stop! You're going to catch my lawn on fire," I shouted. Before I could say more, the sparks died and my rose bushes appeared bursting with blossoms. I shook my head. Was I hypnotized? My jaw hung open and the flowers' rich aroma filled my nostrils and coated my mouth.

"See what I can do," Velnukas chuckled.

He clapped his hands sharply and the yard darkened as if the sun had disappeared behind the clouds. My rose garden looked like it had when I first came outside—filled with aphids and tight, mediocre buds.

"Who are you? A magician?"

"You know who I am and you have to decide how badly you want to win the garden show."

"If you're the devil, then you must want my soul in payment or something. Isn't that how it goes in all those stories?" This was a ridicules conversation and I couldn't believe I was having it. Yet he *did* have a way with roses.

Velnukas shrugged, took a puff and scratched the tip of his nose "It's really up to you to decide. There's so much I could do to help you."

I slowly nodded. I'm not sure if it was in agreement about the garden show or just admitting that I needed all the help I could get. Of course, he assumed that I was agreeing to the "bargain," whatever it might be.

"Look, hurry over to Betsy's Brick-a-Brack," he said. "Go to the back room and, under a pile of old linens, there's a large pottery vase – steel blue, shaped like an urn with curly handles. Buy it! We'll use it for that perfect arrangement."

Everything went just as he predicted. Betsy had forgotten the vase was there and, it was so grimy, she gave it to me for practically nothing. After soaking and scouring, the vase shone with a patina almost like pewter. For the rest of the week, Velnukas stood at my good dining room table, puffed his cheroot, and drew endless diagrams on large sheets of paper. He used a ruler, protractor and compass making me feel like we were back in geometry class.

Watching him wield the compass like a dagger, I worried he'd gouge my table and finally said, "I don't think we need to bother with so many detailed drawings. We're just arranging flowers, you know."

124

"Right," he answered. "You're such an expert at this and you have all those blue ribbons to prove it." That was so mean and snippy. I just shook my head and left the room.

Velnukas made me promise that I'd be awake by 3:00 in the morning on the day of the garden show but the sun was shining in my face when I opened my eyes. I looked at the clock: 5:30! I jumped out of bed, threw on my old terrycloth robe and rushed to the kitchen to make coffee. A full ten-cup carafe was sitting on the warmer and Velnukas was in my dining room surrounded by buckets and buckets of cut roses in a rainbow of hues.

"How did you get in my house?" I yelled at him.

"What does it matter? Get dressed and get to work. We must be finished by nine so you can get it to the show."

I spent the morning jumping around like a marionette, following his detailed and tedious instructions, filling the huge vase with roses, lantanas, and other flowers whose names I didn't know and I'm sure were never in my garden. When I questioned him about that, he snapped: "Of course, they're in your garden by the fence. You never go back there to see what you have."

By nine o'clock, I was looking at the most beautiful flower arrangement I had ever seen. It was like a painting by one of the Dutch masters. "Wow," was all I could say.

Velnukas had a wooden picture frame, gilded with silver, and he set it in front of the flower vase.

"Wait, those little brackets in the back will never hold that heavy frame."

He looked at me and sniffed. Amazingly, the tiny brackets held and the arrangement definitely looked like a fine painting. "I want you to display it just like that," he said and handed me a spray bottle filled with water. "It's a hot day. Mist those flowers every two hours."

At the garden show, my arrangement drew all eyes and towered above the rest. People came to ask how I got different types of roses to open at the same time.

"It took some work and a lot of luck," I mumbled.

Janet stopped and looked it over very closely. She bumped the table and said: "I'm sorry. I almost knocked over your picture frame. It would be a pity to have it knock over your arrangement. Those brackets look too fragile to hold something so big."

"They're strong," I answered.

I won a blue ribbon for the best arrangement and a second blue for the most innovative display. I'd thought I'd be thrilled but I wasn't. No, it wasn't my guilty conscience. In my mind the phrase, "It's only a flower show," echoed over and over again. After the competition, I was packing up when Rev. Beasley, one of the judges, came up to me.

"You know, we had a special award for you this year," he said. "You've been such a good sport all these years that we had this made just for you." He held out a small gold trophy. My name was engraved on the base along with the words: "Hours and flowers soon fade away but the lesson of your perseverance is here to stay."

"I feel foolish giving it to you after your spectacular wins," he said, "but we can't take it back because of the engraving. I thought you might like to have it. The judges always admired your dedication."

I was speechless and clutched the trophy to my heart.

And Velnukas? He returned that evening and demanded my soul in exchange for those blue ribbons. I told him we'd never reached any agreement. We argued all night about who said what, when to whom. I was as stubborn as he was. We finally compromised and decided if I could give him a task he couldn't perform, he'd desist in his demand. He gave me 24 hours to come up with this task. I insisted on a time limit for its completion–whatever task I gave him, should be completed in an hour, not take eternity. He smirked and left.

The hardest day of my life followed. I couldn't imagine anything that would stump a devil and I couldn't go to anyone for advice. How do you bring up the subject without having people think you're really wacky? As the deadline grew near, I sat in the kitchen with my head in my hands. Then it came to me! Something I've always hated about myself might just be my salvation. When Velnukas appeared, I had what looked like a pile of steel wool on the top of the table.

"What's this?" He asked.

"It's my hair. I cut a bunch off and it's the task I've set for you. If you can straighten my hair in an hour, I guess you've won." I turned on my kitchen timer.

He grinned and waved his cheroot. But where the sparks landed, my hair went up in smoke. He grabbed a hunk and pulled and tugged and pressed. The more he tried the curlier it got. He spat on it and stomped on it and the hair turned rusty orange like a curly old Brillo pad. When my timer went "ding," Velnukas was covered in sweat. "This is stupid," he shouted and whirled away.

So did I get the best of the devil or just frustrate a crazy gardener? Who knows? But I can tell you I've never had a great deal of respect for the devil's intelligence. After all, he failed his first and most important IQ test when he lost paradise.

In the weeks that followed, everything changed. I volunteered at the library and at the animal shelter, two places whose doors Janet never darkened. People talked to me more or, maybe, I had more to say to them. Also, I had my rose garden dug up and seeded the yard with grass. A lawn service takes care of it now.

PLANTING PEAS

ODARKA POLANSKYJ STOCKERT

On my birthday, each year,
I like to plant peas
no matter the weather.

Even in a cool drizzle, I rub the earth into my skin
break up the hardened ground
roll the round, rough and green balls in my palm
see them tumble into the furrows.

The days pass, rains come
cold enters the bone
then the heavens open
the gods warm the earth
greening.

The years I don't plant
the summer arrives abruptly
I miss the shooting sprouts
the rains

am thrown headlong into the heat
with no reprieve, no warning.

But when I plant, it's like a year a baby is born
time expands, hours stretch into days broad, full
and teeming.

TURNING FORTY

ELLEN STONE

August has a brittle edge,
a rough beauty that once was lush
like the dry stalks of sweet yarrow
flanking the overgrown garden.
Flaxen fronds of prairie grass
rise above the flower tangle: sun-bleached
purples, brown-edged yellows, rust and sage.
The vibrant husk of summer begins to fade.

There is a sharpness in the air.

Cicadas chirr in the backyard trees.

Their strange rattle rises and falls mid occasional birdsong,
and the soft rustle of still-green leaves from the shagbark hickory.
The twilight chill shrugs me into my sweater, and even in the hammock
beneath the tulip poplar, summer sings a slow, sad song,
the mourning dove's lament:
"What is left to do? What is left to do?"

Morning comes full and round,
tomatoes to pick for sauce, the smell
of basil and garlic simmer through the walls.
Promise bursts through the pot as the fruit
swells and swirls through onion and pepper,
pieces cut up hastily, a handful of parsley
thrown in, the final thought, oregano
plucked carefully from the bloom-filled
stem, an ending note, a prayer
for what is there and what's to come.

HOW TO LEAVE A GARDEN

SHIRLEY SUSSMAN

> *"We must cultivate our garden."*
> –Voltaire

YOU MAY NEVER need to know this. I certainly didn't think I would. But in the name of good sportsmanship, I pass this on.

First you cry, but not near the delphiniums. Their melancholy, stooped, blue spires in no way advocate for their tolerance of salt. Their downright finicky need for full sun, cool temperatures, high humus content, and a neutral *ph*, should argue against their presence in the garden at all. But it doesn't. You probably agree. Some things are worth fussing over.

The young plumbagos, on the other hand, wear their baby blue crowns like they're expecting to be stepped on, spreading willy-nilly past defined borders, low to the ground and underfoot. The more mature plumbagos dare you to remember that their prickly brown seedpods were once as soft as the youngsters they replaced. A few tears won't kill them. Delicate and hardy, I leave them both to you, to fail or thrive without me.

For as many years as it has taken the wanton wisteria to overwhelm the stalwart silver maple, unlucky enough to have been planted too close, I have been friend, midwife, and undertaker to these four acres. If I had done half as well in the house with Richard, I might be there yet. Give me a chrysanthemum, and I know just when to stop pinching back to get the best bloom: a skill I never mastered with my husband.

So: I leave Richard; I leave the house; I leave the garden.

The boxwoods, thank goodness, can take care of themselves. Study them to see how well they manage: 70 years old and still able to regenerate after a hard pruning. The last time I cut out so many yellow and orange cupped-leaf branches—*phytophthera infestans* the extension agent said after I sent him a sample—I wondered if maybe it was finally too much. But it wasn't. The next spring tiny green fingers, sprouting everywhere there was a cut, tickled me back when I ran my hands over their innocent exuberance.

You can practically take the ferns for granted, but don't. Their brave fetal push through last season's seemingly impenetrable carpet of leaves defines hope. Every spring be amazed that their fiddleheads are tough enough to break through. They hoard their strength in tight rolls, and only unfurl to feathery delicacy when they are well past the hardship of their birth. Take note.

If the ferns aren't compelling enough, look to the peonies. Pale, fleshy tips break cover in early spring and break hearts: they are too pink to survive. An oblivious foot, an unrestrained rake or a too heavy hand at weeding reduces the potential of the most sanguine nib. But, like the ferns, they take their strength from their fierce self-centeredness. Only when their heads reach above foot level do they forgive their enemies, and unfurl with mitten-leafed optimism.

And, as if they wouldn't be invited back without a gift for the hostess, they offer up creamy, fat buds, so heavy they can barely lift their heads: certainly too heavy to open by themselves.

So they call for help. Ants.

Do not spray.

The sticky nectar is their reward for releasing a *mille-feuille* of silky petals. Be prepared when the sun-gold stamen draws you ineluctably down to inhale. There is no aroma, except maybe that of the lily-of-the-valley, which is more seductive. Tuck a bloom behind your ear. Richard does not like store-bought perfume.

I leave them to you because I cannot grow where they are. I thought if I nurtured them, they would return the favor. If I didn't cut the daffodil leaves until their bulbs resorbed the lifeblood for next year's flowers, they would shield me. If I cut back the bearded iris in the summer and carefully pulled dirt away from their rot-prone, tuberous chests, they would stand guard for me the following spring. If I divided the astilbes so their pink, red and white plumes had room to toss their pretty heads like young girls who know they are being watched, they would warn me, somehow. But they didn't. I may have been asking too much. It doesn't matter.

I have a confession: there's no excuse for what I did to the clematis. Up to the very end, I lied to myself. Why did I plant five new varieties on the sunny side of the fence, when I wouldn't be around to keep their feet cool with a ground cover? So what if I tied their frail leaders, oh so tenderly, to the uprights? They needed to be under-planted. I knew that. And I acted as if I had all the time in the world, that the searing sun was months away. And it was. But I was long gone by then—except for stealth visits when I knew Richard was out.

They burned. Like babies left out without their bonnets. Crisp. Brown.

I don't deserve to be forgiven for that. But somehow the cosmos and impatiens, one season annuals, don't hold a grudge. A trick neither

Richard nor I ever learned. They reappear on their own in heavily mulched beds, like forgotten deposits growing unexpected dividends. You may wonder why the rest of the annuals stay missing. In my own defense, I left before Mother's Day, the safe frost-free planting date. Weeds have filled in for the zinnias, ageratum and salvia, like unrehearsed understudies. I'm embarrassed to leave such a mess. If you don't mind a suggestion, think about sweet alyssum next to the volcanic rock border. It looks like fairy dust.

The beech was not my fault. The drought was so severe, no matter how many times I moved the hose, the hydrangea or the weeping cherry, or the kousa dogwood stayed too thirsty. The tree surgeon said it was already stressed, that the lindane, toxic as it was, could not recall the invitations the beech had sent out. The bark beetles feasted. There was nothing to be done but use the logs in the woodstove.

That should have been the end, but it wasn't. When the beech came down, sun scalded the yellowwood's previously shaded, forked crotch. And the pachysandra, like supplicants in a church of dappled shade suddenly parish suppressed, couldn't shrivel fast enough. A once lush bed shrank to a few hardy survivors. I've seen some new offshoots this spring. It may come back yet, if you're patient about weeding the vacated spaces; give the new life a chance to take hold.

Inasmuch as I chose to leave, I admit I'm surprised how quickly Richard has replaced me with an exotic variety. I wonder if you'll thrive in foreign soil. I hear you're an accomplished gardener in zone four, but I could probably still give you some pointers for zone seven: how to conserve moisture during the dog days—mulch deeply around the magnolia; how to send roots deeper and wider for nourishment—deep water the sunflowers until they refuse to be uprooted at the end of the season; how to plant next to a sympathetic, concurrently fruiting variety—choose a bird-magnet mulberry tree as a willing martyr for the sour cherry.

But you'll probably want to find out for yourself. You'd mistrust my motives, anyway, as if I'd leave out the secret ingredient in my anti-damping-off potting mixture.

Smell, feel, and taste the dirt, so if you ever have to leave, your nose, fingers, and mouth will remember. There is no substitute for torn-cuticle, broken-nail gardening. You know that. You'll worry holes with your index and middle fingers through every pair of gloves you buy, no matter how durable the label promises. You'll grind through the knees of your pants. And don't become too attached to your tools. You'll lose your trowel in a frenzy of finishings whenever Richard calls you away from your seedlings. To tend to him.

Let it be the morning glories rather than the delphiniums that draw your tears. A bit of salt won't hurt them. Their frail blueness belies their tough, sweet potato vine ancestry. Maybe you already know that the seeds require a twenty-four-hour soak and nicking of their hard seed coat before planting, that their jack-in-the-beanstalk growth pattern is splendid for covering up eyesores.

But there is something else. Someone should warn you.

The most dangerous time will be mid-morning when their pale throats are open so achingly wide, as if their honest vulnerability could stop the inevitable. In an hour their heavenly blue bells will be twisted shut; in a day they will be litter off the vine to be gathered for compost.

Gardeners learn best from experience.

A final tip: you don't really need four acres. Window boxes planted with dusty miller, trailing vinca, and blue salvia can be quite lovely, viewed from a dining table set for one.

And if you add lantana, expect hummingbirds. Call it a party when they sip nectar from their tiny ruby and amethyst pitchers.

POEM FOR A 75TH BIRTHDAY

MARILYN L. TAYLOR

Love of my life, it's nearly evening
and here you still are, slow-dancing
in your garden, folding and unfolding
like an enormous grasshopper in the waning
sun. Somehow you've turned our rectangle
of clammy clay into Southern California,
where lilacs and morning-glories mingle
with larkspur, ladyfern and zinnia,
weaving their way across the loom
of your fingers—bending
toward the trellis of your body
making fabulous displays of their dumb
and utter gratitude, as if they knew
they'd be birdseed if it weren't for you.

And yet they haven't got the slightest clue
about the future; they behave as if
you'll be there for them always, as if you
were the sun itself, brilliant enough
to keep them in the pink, or gold, or green
forever. *Understandable*, I decide
as I look at you out there—as I lean
in your direction, absolutely satisfied
that summer afternoon is all
there is, and night will never fall.

133

134

WEEDING THE LILACS

JAN TREFFER THOMPSON

IT GOES LIKE this: house, yard, lilacs, Highway 40. I had hoped they would be taller by now, these plants I dug from Mom's hedge and drove to my new home, their five-gallon bucket pinched between front and back seats. Seven feet after five years, seed catalogs promise for theirs, but mine still don't hide the road. Even on my knees, I can see clearly over the green-tipped branches and through empty spaces where some have withered and died. The blacktop beyond sparkles in the sun and runs off to the horizon.

Damp earth gives like Play-Doh under the hand that holds me up, collecting under nails I've only started to grow long again. I reach with the other hand and grab, ripping out another clump of tall grass by its roots. Black dirt clings to the ends and I shake it off, into the lilac bed, before tossing the rest into the ditch.

Chad and Keith race by in stiff, new swim trunks, shooting water guns without aim. Cold drops like pellets hit my back and I gasp. "Godammit, keep that water in the pool!" They run laughing back into the plastic ring set up on our front lawn, their hard little bodies already browning at the edges; they soak up sun just like the grass and the dirt and the trees do. What I feel is the last breath of winter in a spring breeze, and the brittle spines of last year's grass that hurt the soft white leg flesh I bare anyway, though it's too early for a tan.

"Kinda young for you, ain't they?" Dave had scowled about the cutoffs, but his eyes shifting nervously under a greasy seed corn cap said different and I looked straight back at him, though my cheeks burned. I could feel it, the hardness I'd been building back up an hour at a time inside my shoulders and thighs, butt and belly. It was there, he could see it and it was Dave who turned away this time, stalking out with only a light kiss on my forehead to say he was going. Where his fingers touched me in that moment there was a shy question, and I liked that. I liked it, too, that I could choose not to answer.

I close my eyes, command my cells to fill with sunshine as they used to on the shadeless pitching mound of a softball field, or on the muddy creek banks where my friends and I would throw down towels and bake ourselves. My insides vibrated then to pounding bass lines from Styx or Def Leppard and I thought that was the rhythm of life. We sang of the best of times, and then about dancin', dancin' in the sheets like we knew what we were talking about. The music drowned out questions we didn't want to ask, the ideas we didn't want to have. I know that now.

Sweat runs like a tick through my hair roots. Splashes and shouts from behind me; the pool is too small to hold both boys, and eventually they'll fight for what's theirs. It's the way with them. I rip at the roots again and again, sifting impatiently through the grass and the bark of the lilac plants, watching for tiny runners I must leave so they can grow tall. But among the stems I see something else, and pull back.

The rattler's skin looks dirty, even now when it's empty. Blood thumping down to my fingertips, I lean forward to see more. It twines through the branches as the snake traveled, knowing the unyielding bark would scratch off what was making him itch and squirm. Not snake but what had been snake; only the impression of scales and hard muscles that still make up the snake who's now sunbathing up the road, or has fled to a cool, dark hole.

Chad's laughter, riding the wind, hits me in the back. I read once that humans slough off millions of cells each day, a whole body's worth every seven years. As my fingers touch the withered snakeskin, I wonder how much of myself I will leave behind.

GARDENING

CLAUDIA VAN GERVAN

Last year I planted in the hard pan.
This year I'm the root digging down.

Last year I railed at empty clouds.
This year I drift like a vapor.

Last year the air was on fire.
This year I swim in the moon.

Rivers give me answers
to the questions I never asked,

Everything lost, buried, panned for
rises up between my toes.

Last year I scratched for a living.
This year I'm itchy with luck.

PERENNIAL GARDEN

DIANALEE VELIE

In my final garden,
I will wear an evening gown
of eyelet and snow
and a necklace of shiny stars.
The night sky, dressed in formal tuxedo,
will be my constant companion.
My finger tips will touch the sun
and I will catch rain water in my hair
offering the moon a drink of nectar
from my chalice,
a slice of fruit from my womb.

In my final garden,
peonies will pen poetry,
hydrangeas will harmonize,
tulips will tap dance,
and the willows will sway
in syncopated rhythm,
as the universe steals me away
in a flaming chariot after handing
me one perfect white rose,
proclaiming:

"Such joy to be planted
in The Perennial Garden this Spring."

FARM SENTINEL

MARY KUYKENDALL-WEBER

LIFE NOT ONLY changed for all us when my father died, but the farm seemed to lose its will to live, too. The corn he had planted a month before was still trying to shoot its way up through the dir,t even though he had thoroughly cultivated and pulverized the soil. There had been plenty of rain although nothing like the downpour on the day he died. He had gotten all of his sun-cured hay in the barn just before it hit. He was so attuned to nature that other farmers used to do as he did....they had been only an hour behind him in getting their hay in.

It was when my mother checked the barn to find out why he was late for supper that she found him beside the tractor. It was still running...something was wrong...he would never waste gas. She saw the new breeding bull he had gotten attached to; it had belonged to his uncle in the next county who had given up farming because he could no longer compete with the big corporate feedlots in the West. The big Hereford was nuzzling him gently, trying to get my father to move. My mother saw his face was peaceful but lifeless. She knew his weak heart was probably the cause.

She called for Mike, my brother. He was sharpening the blades on the mowing machine. My two sisters and I were in the house with our aunts and uncles. Once a year, we would get together for a reunion of those born on the farm. The farm had given us our start in life. When our ancestors settled the valley in the 1740s, there had been plenty of land to support the first three generations. But large families resulted in too many heirs and, thus, smaller farms. So the English rule had been adopted for the past three generations. The farm would go to the eldest son, or, barring that, to the son that wanted to stay on the farm. The farm would educate the others so they could make a living. It was true that it had to be mortgaged to get my oldest sister through the state university, a comedown from the prior generation when it had even sent my father's sisters through expensive finishing schools.

I was lucky that four years separated me from my oldest sister. She not only paid off the mortgage but managed to loan me the money to also go to the state university. My middle sister went to a nearby free nursing college.

Our mother had married our father when they were just 18, both graduating from the same high school class. Mike had been their only son so it was automatic that he would inherit the farm. He did his duty and had even enhanced his reputation for working hard by becoming known for his mechanical ability. He worked part-time at the local machinery dealership to supplement the decreasing farm income. Because of the high cost of farm equipment, the valley farmers had begun sharing equipment such as combines. Mike's instinctive sense of coming rain gained him the reputation my father had first earned.

During the past two generations, the farm had supported the education of a chemist, an engineer, a nurse, several teachers and a lawyer with one son staying behind to run the farm. If any of us were ever frustrated in our jobs, we shared this with each other and not the one left to run the farm. Any complaints we had would sound pretty trite in comparison to the never-ending chores and risks a farmer faces.

When my mom and brother, Mike, came in with the horrible news that my father was dead, we couldn't believe it. My two sisters and I had not even seen him this visit as all of us had arrived that afternoon. We had planned on walking the fields with them the next day just to hear how things were going, a ritual that was good for all of us to connect with our past, as providers and beneficiaries. While my mother called the doctor, my sisters and I just looked at each other, stunned. Somehow we felt the farm, Daddy, Mom and Mike had become indestructible....something we could always come home to. All of us rushed to the barn to gather around my father until the doctor and coroner came. I mostly remember the bull that had been nudging my father. Mike had tied the animal to a nearby hay bin; the sounds of his grazing seemed soothing. Yet, he would pause to look over at my father with those huge, dark, unblinking eyes.

Over the next couple of months, the lawyer on my father's side of the family would be called upon to help. It turned out my father had not made social security payments for two hired hands. He had given both his and their contributions directly to them, figuring they would spend it more wisely than the government. Then it was discovered the farm, because it was so close to Washington, DC, had tripled in value. It was being taxed on commercial value rather than farm income. The lawyer in our family as well as many others had been trying to get this rule changed, which did result in a Tax Reform Act. The act based a farm's value on the income it produced, not what it would be worth for commercial development. But it didn't go into effect until a year after my father died. So it was too late for my brother, Mike. To keep the farm, the cattle herd and the farm equipment had to be sold to pay the taxes on a farm now valued at $500,000 instead of $25,000. So Mike went to work as a truck driver, which paid better than working on farm equipment at the local dealer.

We went back to our jobs. Mom turned the farm over to our cousin, one of the few farmers still left with a herd and equipment, asking him only to pay the property taxes, knowing that was about all he could make on the land.

Then a near tragedy struck again, just three months after our father's death. Mike had come home from driving the truck to repair a neighbor's tractor and his arm had gotten caught in the power takeoff mechanism. If he had not been wearing Daddy's old jacket, which ripped easily, he could have lost his arm or his life.

He and my mother had no sooner come back from the hospital that evening when two tractor trailers loaded with lean cattle arrived with a bill for $8,000. Daddy had cut back on developing his own small herd because he could make more money turning the pasture into corn fields and using the silage to fatten them up during the winter. Hillside farmers did not have this advantage and eked out a living by selling their new heifers in the fall because they couldn't store enough hay to feed them. Daddy had not told my mother that he had ordered this fall's shipment of lean cattle.

141

The driver helped Mom get them penned up in the barnyard while Mike did what he could with one arm. They had just gotten the gates fastened when I arrived, having heard about Mike's accident earlier that day. We would have to work something out to fatten the cattle. The corn crop, though not good, had grown and maybe would produce enough silage to fatten them. Otherwise, it would be a huge financial loss as my brother simply could not, in his condition, handle that many cattle. Besides, he could not afford to lose his job. He was married and had one child with one on the way. A resale of the cattle as is would only bring half the value at most, a loss of $4,000.

While we were calming ourselves down at the kitchen table, trying to find a positive side, we could hear the restless cattle in the barnyard. This was not unusual since they were adjusting to new surroundings. Mike had noticed that several in the herd suffered from what Daddy called shipping fever because they were sweaty, frothing at the mouth, and hard to control. Mom had gotten the reluctant driver to herd the ailing ones inside the barn.

We had just managed to believe that possibly we could maybe even make a little money on the deal if our cousin and other relatives in the valley could feed the cattle until it was time to take them to the stock sale in February. The corn had not been harvested. But all of us could take whatever vacation we had now to cut the corn and fill the silo. We could take turns coming home on weekends and any other days we could get off to help our mother, cousin and other relatives in the valley feed the cattle during the week.

It was then we saw the spotlight from a car on the road sweep the fields. It was illegal to jack deer at night by stunning them with a spotlight, making them easy to shoot. My mother jumped up to the phone to call the game warden about the illegal deer poachers. The deer were in the field just below the barn. The hunters were out of their cars now shooting wildly, and Mike was quickly on his feet as the sound of gun shots seemed to be coming around the house and barn. But it was too late. We both heard the nervous cattle stampeding. Not only did the 60 steers in the yard break through the gate but the sick ones in the barn busted out of the side of the 100-year-old barn when a gun shot went into it.

They were running in circles in the 25-five acre pasture field. It was a night with just a quarter-moon and I could see some of the darting, whirling white markings on the Herefords. Most of the cattle were black, Angus. All I could see of them were running shapes. The ground was shuddering as they thundered around the field. You could hear them breathing hard and loud, losing pounds. We had just been talking about adding fat to the cattle and knew that they were losing weight now as they stampeded. We had to get them back into the barnyard where they could settle down and eat. Mom got in the truck to go to the neighbors for help.

The deer jackers with spotlights had gone, perhaps realizing what they had done by shooting so close to the barn. Mike was able to get up on the tractor and get it to the end of the field where he used its lights to back light me so I could see where I was going. I tried driving the cattle to the gate they had broken through but they simply would not settle down and quit running. Mike and I began mimicking my father's soothing sounds. I could hear Mike's voice crack as his broken ribs were no doubt hurting him. He had gotten off the tractor to stand guard in one end of the field but simply could not keep up with the cattle. The slivered moon threw reflected light off the white bandages around his ribs and arm.

Darting back and forth, I could feel Mike's relief as the dark Angus shadows and white-faced Herefords headed towards the broken gate. We dared not speak as noise would spook them. Then another gun shot rang out further down the valley. All I could feel was the ground shaking under me as the mass of black and white came thundering towards me. I couldn't speak, hear or even move. I just felt the earth, the movement of the cattle towards me. They were pushing memories, all rushing through me. It seemed like my father was just ahead of them. He seemed to be there in the dark night.

Then I knew what he would do. I had to stand straight up no matter what. If I fell the stampeding herd would not see me. I would be crushed under their feet, pulverized, swallowed by the earth. Did my ancestors want me, would the farm take me, would it like me, use me? I could smell and feel their heavy breath as the cattle came straight at me. Then I felt the farm, my father, the growing fields. I reached up just like withered corn did when raindrops began to fall. I was being whip-lashed by the cattle as they began to divide around me and close in behind me. But I didn't fall. It seemed to last a lifetime but I stood tall. *As tall as my father*, I said to myself as I reached up even further. I could still see the shapes of the tall corn in the field next to me as the cattle thundered around and by me. I was still motionless when I heard them behind me.

The cattle were turning again but not towards me. Mike's white bandage was moving and I heard his pain as he struggled up behind them. He had seen that I was safe. The cattle were heading to the river side of the field next to the cornfield. Mike quickly signaled me to close in along the back side so they would follow the fence. The fence led to the broken gate. They followed it. They found the opening. Amazingly they went through.

Mike and I were right behind them. I propped the broken gate back up and Mike brought the tractor up against it to secure it. I looked at the slivered moon hanging just above the cornfield. Back then, corn was not planted by drilling it in rows to get more corn. Seeds were drop-planted in hills so it could be tilled and weeded from two directions. Thus, from every vantage point, you could see the corn standing tall, in perfect harmony, advancing up and down the field. The corstalksn now seemed to be moving in lockstep like soldiers, marching, watching us. I felt my father was there with others before him.

We watched as the cattle settled down in the barnyard, now munching on our best timothy hay strewn around the barnyard by my mother who had arrived with help. Somehow I knew the farm would be there for the next generation. It was still alive. It had saved me. I hoped I could return the favor.

FIRST CROCUS

ANTHONY RUSSELL WHITE

Delicate old-lady's-hat purple
streaking through translucent white.
But only a child would have put
bright orange at the center.
This combination, this early arrival,
says, expect the miraculous.
Expect tiny chapels found in fox dens,
new songs that make men fall down and weep,
children born with stars on their foreheads,
claw marks at your door.

144

MIÈA'S GARDEN

MARIANNE WOLF

MIÈA'S GARDEN IS a community composed of dozens of species all integral
to the survival of the habitat. Like ethnic neighborhoods forming an urban
city, these species without maps, from the simplicity of the daisy to the
spectacular Oriental poppy, have settled in one corner or another of the
broad landscape that for seven months of the year consumes Mièa's
imagination.

For as long as she could remember, Mièa always wanted a garden.
It was a hunger she felt, something missing from her life that could feed
her middle-aged soul, open up her mind, and let her drift endlessly in a
refuge from her real life as she knelt on the earth, dug her fingers into the
dirt and felt the possibilities.

145

Each April, she waits for the first signs of new green shoots. Just
as in a painter's palette, there are hundreds of different shades of green in
Mièa's garden. Mièa wonders how God chose which greens would go with
which blossom colors when, as a homeowner, it took her days to select a
shade of white.

As invitations to Mother Nature's open house, from spring until
the first frost, she's posted new foliage of various shapes, sizes, and
textures in the garden to lure butterflies, birds, insects, and the occasional
human, all tourists, to this part of her perennial beds.

In botanical terms, perennials are non-woody plants that return
year after year, requiring no replanting. At the end of each growing season,
they die down then reappear at the start of the next. Those that are hardy
can withstand Chicago's freezing temperatures. There are a few, though
technically perennials, which are too tender for the winters in the
midwestern climate zone and end up like annuals.

Mièa often looks at her garden filled with its flourishing plants
and creatures and wonders how it must feel to know the season is about
to change, to know that soon the beautiful petals and leaves will shrivel
into decaying compost. Mièa wonders what it must be like to know it's
almost time to journey south or west or burrow deep inside the earth to

hibernate. She marvels at the process they will undertake to re-seed themselves, to push their roots deep enough to withstand a topsoil freeze. Mièa wonders how God thought this all up. How did God plan which flowers would have to be replanted with each new spring? Why do some survive and regroup to be more beautiful as well as fuller, taller, or stronger than in their first season?

When Mièa first planted her backyard garden, it was barely a garden at all but more like patches of plants where there wasn't concrete or wood. There was a towering oak tree that she guessed to be more than 60 years old but badly decomposing. She'd discovered that someone, likely an idiot handling tools, had hammered a copper nail into it. Slowly the tiny hole had hollowed out and grown to an oversized wound. A convenient place where raccoons or squirrels would most likely climb to nest, it was close to the house. The right gust of wind could easily bring the old oak crashing on the rooftop of her two-story Tudor or her aging garage.

The decision had been made to cut the tree down before it fell. Its trunk reduced to bits of sawdust, part of its root system dug up and dissected from the earth, the remaining roots continue to die out and turn into rich fertilizer for what has become Mièa's perennial garden.

146

Mièa would like a conversation with God. She wants to understand why that oak had to be destroyed. Had the tree been left alone though, she wouldn't drift with the serenity found among the flowers, foliage, and animals in her backyard. As the caretaker of this garden, she's constantly amazed how one plant or creature's life cycle contributes to another species' survival. On those occasions Mièa's hushed to silence for the process she slowly witnesses with each new day.

It is early May and Mièa waits in her corner of the world for what she terms "vacationers on holiday" to visit during the brief spring, if any, and see which will stay throughout the summer. The perennials have returned and grown tall enough for her to recognize where the autumn winds blew last summer's seeds.

Last spring to attract butterflies, Mièa had labored on boney knees with mud clinging to her skin to plant 'Lady Stratheden,' Geum Chiloense (qullyon) with its yellow/orange petals next to the steps of her deck. This spring, to her surprise, she feels the plant's energy as it runs rampant along the border of her driveway and heads west into the 'White Nancy.' How does Mièa explain why three small plantings of Stachys (byzantina) turned into massive clusters of what appear to resemble gray-white, furry lamb's or rabbit's ears along the entire driveway? Like the animal, the plant increases rapidly; single foliage spreads forming a clump with flower stems bearing miniature leaves tipped by small swirls of purple flowers.

In her naiveté, Mièa attempted to keep the colors separated. The master gardener knew better. Now blended together, the hues are even more striking.

With the warming temperatures and the aid of spring showers, the varied vegetation forms new shapes. The hybrid tea rose Mièa thought was dead has pushed up suckers now twice the size of the original foliage. These branches fill with leaves and buds stretched towards the sun; they create arches over the mix of foliage below it. Its neighbor are the poppies; these slender stems, abundant with large buds soon to burst into delicate flowers, will resemble crinkled blood orange silk.

Far from uniform in their appearance, each plant's leaves are unique. While some have fine green feathering, others are thickly furred, and some look smooth as though they've been polished to reflect the sun. For Mièa, the comparisons between plant forms and human adaptation are abundant.

Many of the garden plants have an apparent elegance with sweeping stems. A patch of Solomon's Seal, polygonatum (ordoratum) 'Variegatum,' has broad oval leaves with white margins; each arranged perfectly on both sides of the stem and nearly in horizontal planes. A miniature shaped bell blossom hangs suspended by short threadlike stalks joined at each leaf. These stems have always appeared to Mièa as wedding bells hung in preparation for a bug wedding. Under the archway, a set of small holes is revealed, maybe for a worm or a field mouse, or a bug. Mièa imagines these as the entrance for a new home of bug newlyweds.

147

Tangled by the foliage of the overgrown clematis, her heart pounds at the animal tracks she uncovers and Mièa realizes she's not aware of what's been burrowing between the Russian Sage. Her heart thumps as her eyes scan the ground. She wonders, if she keeps still, will whatever it is come out? Mièa doesn't want to miss what her garden attracts.

Certain flowers, she knows, attract birds. As a child, Mièa used to keep parakeets as pets. They were her playmates, angels with whom she'd share her secrets and sorrows. Now to her delight, patches of daisies, coreopsis, lanceolate, sage, salvia, lamiaceae, and 'Crater Blue Lake,' Veronica (austriaca teucrium) attract dozens of feathered species into her backyard.

Not unlike the Three Stooges, a trio of blue jays dive bombs the yard from high atop the towering evergreens and maples in the neighborhood. In those surrounding trees are house finches, sparrows, woodpeckers, starlings, grackles, pairs of cardinals, families of mourning doves, and even two wayward pigeons. All of these feathered creatures have made Mièa's yard their turf.

She scans the treetops as the birds sing melodies only they can fully understand. She watches as they take turns flying in and landing on a bird feeder in the outermost corner of the yard. Certain birds land on the perches of the feeder and use their beaks to toss seeds to the ground for the other members of their flock.

It's this obvious pecking order within each species, and with each other, that Mièa's most curious to watch. Pairs of crested head cardinals are the first diners each morning and the last every evening. From her kitchen windows Mièa watches the male with his black masked eyes and bright red plumage stand guard over his nondescript brown mate, who all but blends into the shrubs. This pair, she knows, has built its nest of bulky twigs and tree bark in the evergreens along the north side of the house. Mièa often pauses to listen when she hears the male call and his mate answers. She's touched by the devotion of the birds to each other and aches when she hears the lonely haunting melody the cardinal sings in earnest searching the neighborhood when his mate is missing.

But it's the squirrels that are the neighborhood's hoodlums. Each year a family of brown-furred rascals lives high in the tree bordering Mièa's yard. She's found them on unusually hot days sprawled out in their fur coats against the shady spots of the deck, against the cool concrete of the garage, or flat in the dirt beneath the peony bushes.

148

They are fearless of her and will stand on their hind legs in front of the kitchen door placing their paws together as if in prayer for peanuts when hungry; they shimmy their tails from side to side, in a sort of cha-cha to entertain Mièa. She shakes her head, letting out a girlish laugh as the squirrels step closer to peer through the glass. She thinks it's uncanny how their eyes meet hers and they appear to smile.

Mièa also knows these same squirrels bully the feeding birds by flinging their limber bodies up from the ground, and flying five feet through the air to scatter the birds. In mid-air, paws stretch out to grasp then cling onto any edge of the birdfeeder...all for a sunflower seed.

While hanging upside down, the squirrels use their free limbs to scoop paws full of seeds they don't care to eat and drop them to the dirt below. Mièa no longer wonders why the pigeons like it in her yard so much! She's often chased a squirrel off the feeder while talking out loud to the birds, "If you'd only organize and gang up, you could chase the squirrels away yourselves." But they perch on the telephone wire and watch and wait for her to refill their birdfeeder.

All of them, each species, are here to remind Mièa who belongs on this land. She may own the house, but their ancestors lived on the property tax-free long before Mièa ever moved to Beverly.

They are her muses. They enlighten her imagination, keep her grounded andcontinually show Mièa the importance of getting along with the neighbors. They need her to watch out for them in this urban insanity as much as Mièa needs them to remind her of who she really is in this life.

This garden makes Mièa think of something else as she bends over, brow furrowed, and plants future bouquets of flowers. Each act sparks her creativity, exposing her to consider her place on the planet and make peace with herself. To soak it all in, accept the energy and understand her garden is the life cycle of more than her imagination: this is real; she is real. Mièa straightens up to stand and focus on her own energy and to slowly breathe it all in. She doesn't want to miss a thing.

149

POPPIES

SALLIE WRIGHT

I

Eager, expectant
every day I inspect their green perfection:
buds
flawlessly formed as bird's eggs.

One day they are green
ova

each bearing a small slit drawn
like a scar;
then they erupt, their crushed
crimson silk,
commanding as an autumn
sunset flushing the sky, black
stamens alert to stain
the rapist.

II

In a moment of total happiness
I tremble at the sight of this
profusion,
this profligate beauty–
right here in my life,
marking the earth on which I live
with exultation.

ONCE I THOUGHT I'D BE A GARDENER

PAULA ANNE YUP

I'd water, weed and put seeds in soil
with my capable body
tackle a community garden
Cape Cod my watering hole
endless weeds I'd pull whenever I could
the dirt between my toes I'd hose off
young and somewhat sweet
and somewhat bitter from a rough start
hard work to throw away
rocks from the dirt

ONCE PASSION

PEGGY ZABICKI

You wonder where Passion has gone.
That flower was here with us
Once.
She grew unattended and wild
Because there was no
Gardener.

Like English Ivy surrounding us,
We watched her grow
From your ivory tower
Until Passion browned and crumbled
Under the harshness of your
Shame and Embarrassment.

Some of the choking vine died.
I would have died for you
Once.
Now there is not enough
Passion for that.
She lies dormant in her winter place far away

ABOUT TALLGRASS WRITERS GUILD

TallGrass Writers Guild is open to all who write seriously at any level. The Guild supports members by providing performance and publication opportunities via its multi-page, bi-monthly newsletter, open mics, formal readings, annual anthologies, and the TallGrass Writers Guild Performance Ensemble programs.

In affiliation with Outrider Press, TallGrass produces its annual "Black-and-White" anthologies, the results of international calls for themed contest entries. Cash prizes and certificates awarded result from the decisions of independent judges.

The Guild is a rarity among arts organizations in that it neither seeks nor accepts federal funding because of the creative limitations imposed by such grants, often of an arbitrary and political nature. For more information on TallGrass Writers Guild membership and programs, call 219-322-7270 or toll-free at 1-866-510-6735. Email tallgrassguild@sbcglobal.net .

ABOUT THE JUDGE

Prophetic, candid, rigorously philosophical, Marvin Bell, winner of numerous awards and fellowships, is an internally acclaimed poet and essayist perhaps best known for his groundbreaking "Dead Man" poems. *Publishers Weekly* says these show "a poet progressing to the peak of his powers, from which the 'sounds of the Resurrected Dead Man's Footsteps' continue to issue full force." His distinctive voice has imprinted the poetic landscape for over four decades.

ABOUT THE EDITOR

Whitney Scott plays many roles in Chicago's literary scene. She is an author, editor, book designer and reviewer whose poetry, fiction and creative nonfiction have been published internationally, earning her listings in *Contemporary Authors* and *Directory of American Poets and Fiction Writers.*

A member of the Society of Midland Authors, she performs her work at colleges, universities, arts festivals and literary venues throughout the Chicago area and has been featured as guest author in the Illinois Authors Series at Chicago's Harold Washington Library. Scott regularly reviews books for the American Library Association's *Booklist* magazine.

Hally Dunn*Financial Advisor
hdunn@royalaa.com
708.456.9122 x 15

AIG ADVISOR GROUP
7234 W. NORTH AVENUE
ELMWOOD PARK, IL 60707

Royal Alliance Associates, Inc.
Securities offered through Royal Alliance Advisors, Inc.
Member NASD, SIPC and AIG Advisor Group

goran coban salon

936 W. Diversey Pky, 2nd Floor, Chicago IL 60614
773-248-0077
gorancoban.com / goran@gorancoban.com

Goran Cobanovoski

154

THE UPTOWN WRITER'S SPACE IS A
MEMBERSHIP BASED ORGANIZATION
DEDICATED TO PROVIDING WRITERS
OF ALL GENRES AN IDEAL WORK
ENVIRONMENT, A SUPPORTIVE
COMMUNITY, OPPORTUNITIES TO
PERFORM THEIR WORK AND TO
HONE THEIR CRAFT, AND MOST
IMPORTANTLY COFFEE AND SNACKS.

Uptown Writer's Space
A WORKSPACE FOR WRITERS

4802 N. BROADWAY
SUITE #200
CHICAGO, IL 60640
WWW.UPTOWNWRITERSSPACE.COM
INFOR@UPTOWNWRITERSSPACE.COM
773-275-1000

Mommy Machine
Kathleen M. McElligott

Baby Boomer Elaine McElroy reinvents herself, leaving behind a failed romance with a younger man and a house that hasn't been remodeled since the Korean War.. She creates a new life for herself in Santa Fe New Mexico, only to be knocked off course when she must raise her toddler grandson alone.

New! From Heliotrope Press

For Order Information: heliotropepress@aol.com

155

Best Wishes to Outrider Press & TallGrass Writers

The Paper Work Place
...for all your editing/word processing needs

2166 Maple Road
Homewood, IL 60430

708-799-1133

Prickly Beer & Purple Panties

selected poems
by Lylanne Musselman

Send $8.00 to 336 N. Graham Avenue
Indianapolis, IN 46219
317.432.8477
more info at http://www.myspace.com/lylanne

Wholesale/Retail

Allen Landscape Centre

1502 Lincoln Hwy.
Schererville, IN 46375
219.865.6181

156

Ascott Window Tinting

Residential ❖ Commercial

Reduces Fading

Scott Johnson
219.363.9367
Since 1986

Controls Heat
Gain & Glare

JOLIET - A historical book by
MARIANNE WOLF

From the Images of America Series
of Arcadia Publishing
www.arcadiapublishing.com

128 pages $19.99   ISBN: 0738540420

Marianne Wolf is a Vice President of the
Illinois Women's Press Association and
Secretary of the TallGrass Writers Guild.
www.mariannewolf.com

The Dancin' Nancys
Acoustic Roots Rock

Booking:

www.thedancinnancys.com

JAN
AS
POETRY

CAROL
AS
NOISE

157

"WORDS ARE ELECTRIC,
BUT NOT ALWAYS STATIC
FREE!"

poetryinnoise@aol.com

*"My art is primarily a thought turned abstract,
I am an individual entity that belongs to no movement."*

Jan Flexon
Artist

19 N. Layman Ave., StudioB
Indianapolis, IN 46219.

Resident Artist @ www.studioschoolgallery.com

____ **A Walk Through My Garden**–$20.50
Writings on crocuses, composting, digital gardens and more _____

____ **Vacations: the Good, the Bad & the Ugly** – $19.50
Writings on respites from stolen moments to Roman holidays _____

____ **Falling in Love Again** – $19.50
Writings on revisiting romance, beloved locales and more _____

____ **Family Gatherings** – $19.50
Writings on families _____

____ **Take Two — They're Small** – $19.50
Writings on food _____

____ **A Kiss Is Still A Kiss** – $18.50
Writings on romantic love _____

____ **Earth Beneath, Sky Beyond** – $18.50
An anthology on nature and our planet _____

158

____ **Feathers, Fins & Fur** – $17.50
Writings on animals _____

____ **Freedom's Just Another Word** – $16.50
Poetry, fiction and essay on freedom _____

____ **Alternatives: Roads Less Travelled** – $16.50
Writings on counter-culture lifestyles _____

____ **Prairie Hearts** – $16.50
Short fiction and poetry on the Heartland _____

____ **Dancing to the End of the Shining Bar** – $10.95
A novel of love and courage _____

Add s/h charges:
$3.95 for 1 book...$5.95 for 2 books...
$1.95 each additional book _____

Send Check or $ Order to:
Outrider Press, Inc.   **Total** ════
2036 North Winds Drive
Dyer, IN 46311

outriderpress@sbcglobal.net